A Year Ou

E.M. Phillips

For my Brother

Flt/Lt Peter Forrow, RAF

who left the party much too soon

Cover design: Graeme Phillips

A Year Out of Time

E.M. Phillips

A Year Out of Time

First published 1995 by TWM Publishing.
This extended edition published 2007.

Published by Sagittarius Publications
62 Jacklyns Lane, Alresford, Hampshire SO24 9LH
Tel: 01962 734322

Typeset by John Owen Smith

ISBN 978-0-9555778-0-2

Printed and bound by CPI Antony Rowe, Eastbourne

Contents

Illustrations by the Author

Introduction

Fifty years after the end of WW2, when Newspapers, Television and Schools alike were washed with a great tide of nostalgia, I found myself bombarded by my grandchildren for wartime artefacts for classroom projects and displays. Desk drawers, trunks and cardboard boxes were ransacked for Ration Books, Identity Cards and photographs; my memory scoured for stories of what it was like to be an evacuee, a subject I privately thought had been done to death in the intervening years, when whole shelves of Public Libraries were crammed with harrowing tales of the misery of children forced to live away from home in alien and sometimes hostile environments. This I am sure was true for some, perhaps most, but as one child for whom evacuation provided perhaps twenty percent sheer terror and a whopping great eighty percent of pure joy, I felt the need to put the record straight; to show the other side of the coin.

The outcome of my efforts was some 2,000 words of reminiscence on the pleasures and pains of being a wartime evacuee, but in some mysterious way that I have never quite fathomed the 2,000 words grew to 3,500 and became a winning short story in a competition sponsored by a local radio station. As a result I was invited to speak in several schools and, urged on by the enthusiastic producer of the Arts programme on the then Wey Valley Radio, now Delta Radio, the 3,500 words rapidly became 15,000 and an eight part weekly radio serial was born.

But before all this happened I took a journey back in time to where it all began: to a small, very small hamlet on the borders of Shropshire and Worcestershire, to refresh my memory and see what, if anything, had changed over the years.

Very little had, it seemed. Roads were perhaps a little wider and busier, hay no longer turned by hand and tossed impossibly high on horse drawn carts, but cut and rolled from a machine in great rectangular bales. There was electric light and central heating and a new village hall, and the water that came from the hills and made even wartime soap produce a luxurious lather was the same: so soft that it lingers like silk on the skin.

Now sixty years on from my first drowsy awakening in a small room under the eves of a village Inn, memory has again been plundered; the story grown to its full length and my year out of time completed.

In the Beginning

As a restricted, nicely brought up child of the 'thirties, I longed for two things: freedom and to be a boy. In retrospect I suppose to have achieved one out of two wasn't bad.

I had no thought at the time that the outbreak of war would bring to an end my safe and relatively peaceful childhood. That for my generation war would bring undreamed of changes: in society, in manners and morals, in how we lived and thought and behaved; in nineteen thirty-nine all that was still in the future.

On the eve of Neville Chamberlain's expected announcement that Great Britain was at war with Germany, and following the instructions left by my sailor father for just such an emergency, my mother, brother and myself travelled by hired car from our home in the peaceful Essex village of Woodford Green to the presumably safer environs of Clacton-on-Sea.

We did have a car of our own but despite all my father's efforts to teach her my mother didn't drive. On the few occasions when she did take the wheel she was absolutely fine until any pedestrians came in sight, when she would head straight for them. This made my father understandably nervous and he made her promise never to try driving again unless he was there to grab the wheel at any threatened emergency. So when we made the momentous move to Clacton the car stayed in the garage and Mr West from the funeral parlour drove us there in his very nice Daimler.

Despite all the excitement and drama of packing, when it came to actually leaving the big old house that backed onto the Epping Forest I couldn't help snivelling a bit at all we were leaving behind: the gate at the end of the garden that allowed us access to the forest beyond; the rustic revolving summer house whose windows and rafters were draped with cobwebs and the silky cocoons of butterfly and moth, and where we left illicit crumbs of cake and biscuit for visiting field mice; the swing, not one of those soulless modern affairs of tubular steel but a proper one, with tall wooden uprights and thick ship's rope, upon the seat of which my brother and I would stand upright, face to face and work it together until we were almost horizontal to the top bar and could see right over the fences into all the gardens along our stretch of the green. Reaching the absolute zenith of our curve there would be a wonderful heart-stopping moment when the seat hung juddering on its ropes before we were sent swooping back down again towards earth, leaving our stomachs stuck somewhere around the treetops.

This was a highly dangerous, totally forbidden and therefore exhilarating pastime only indulged in when my mother was busy in any part of the house where the windows didn't over-look the garden. Now we were saying goodbye to all that. My brother didn't snivel but he was very quiet during the long journey and didn't once deadhead my arm or give me a Chinese burn, so I knew he must be feeling pretty awful about leaving too.

Quite why my parents thought the South East Coast would prove any safer than the Epping Forest in the event of an invasion I can't imagine. But as no adult ever troubled to explain their reasons for any action, however bizarre or unlikely, I at least remained in happy ignorance of why we were to stay with my Aunt Emily and Uncle Leonard.

Aunt Emily was my top favourite out of all my four aunts, she was young and pretty and full of fun. Ever since I could remember, our long summer holidays had been spent with her in the rambling bungalow close to the ornamental gardens and the sea, the only exception being one year when my father was home on leave and rented a cottage at nearby Frinton. This had roses around the door, a very whiffy cesspit and a steep narrow staircase with a sharp twist beneath a lethal overhanging beam. On the first morning my father knocked himself out on this beam and my mother told us we were *never* to repeat to anyone the words he said when he woke up again. They didn't mean a thing to me and I would have forgotten them anyway if my brother hadn't said he knew what they meant and told me. I didn't understand even then, but stored them in my head as something important and interesting and on my return from holiday repeated them in the classroom during Nature Study. Not only were my hands well and truly whacked by the headmistress with her long ruler, but my mother had also to suffer a harrowing meeting with the same terrifying female to discuss my precocious depravity, for which ordeal she unfairly blamed my father when it was really all my brother's fault.

* * * * *

My aunt hated the name Emily, preferring to be called Peggy, but for some reason my mother insisted on using her sister's given name. This I found very confusing and for a time avoided calling her anything at all, then got my legs slapped by my mother for being rude. So I called her Aunt Emily until I was about fourteen, when at her request we dropped both Aunt and Emily altogether and she became Peggy to me for the rest of her long life.

In contrast to my aunt, Uncle Leon was a quiet man who had been in the first war and had caught something called TB in the trenches. This was a mysterious complaint, always spoken about in our hearing in the same hushed tones as some female relative being in a Certain Condition or a neighbour's daughter turning out to be No Better Than She Ought To Be.

11

Consequently my brother and I assumed tuberculosis to belong amongst the many unmentionables and treated poor uncle Leon with a somewhat nervous respect and caution; but as a bank manager he was probably used to that.

Apart from the initial excitement of the air raid sirens sounding within minutes of Chamberlain's speech, for weeks nothing at all happened. I started at the small primary school a short distance from our temporary home and spent all my free time on the beach. It was quite strange to roam the shore out of season and have so much empty sand and sea to explore. By the beginning of October there were no ice-cream parlours or esplanade cafés open, the windows of the gaily-painted beach huts were boarded, the ballroom and rides on the long pier closed for the season; the pier a mere ghost of its summer self. Only the amusement arcade remained open for anyone with the pennies to feed the banks of slot machines. Most of these were one-armed bandits that ate your money and occasionally disgorged a few pennies in return, or those with a mechanical grab you hopefully manipulated for watches and dolls and tin cars but only received a few stale jellybeans for your cash. But there were others which could tell your fortune or stamp your name on a piece of tin, and a half-dozen absolutely marvellous ones where you could, for the modest sum of one penny, watch Lady Jane Grey's head leave her neck, see Marat stabbed in his bath by Charlotte Corday, or witness Guy Fawkes stretched to twice his length on the rack. The best of all these grisly delights I would leave until last, namely a plague cart rumbling along piled high with bodies covered in suppurating plague sores.

What the Butler Saw and *Naughty Parisian Nights* I left to my brother. I didn't spend my pocket money on *that* sort of rubbish.

But by November my mother was becoming restless. She was a woman who liked always to be on the move and doing things. Until we had settled in our present house she had upped and moved every year or so. Never very far so that we had to change school or lose our friends, just simply because she liked moving, though what fun that could have been with two children and an absent husband I can't now imagine. My poor father never knew what he was coming home to and once when he'd been on an extra long trip, found he'd missed out on one house completely.

Anyway, as time passed and no enemy planes had bombed Woodford Green or German tanks rumbled along the Clacton-on-Sea promenade, and no men in grey uniforms had pointed guns at us saying "For you the var iss ovfer", after a further week or two of the phoney war we returned home.

I was bitterly disappointed. Back at school and once again under the eagle eye of a headmistress whom my father had once quite rightly likened to Jane Eyre's Mr Brocklehurst in drag, I seethed with righteous indignation at the unpredictability and downright untrustworthiness of the Germans in general and Hitler in particular. What kind of war was this, I wondered bitterly, when nothing happened and everything was as boringly predictable as ever? The only bright spot in the whole disappointing business was that my mother was too distracted by the news that my father's ship had been commandeered for convoy duties to care what was in my half-term report.

However, we didn't have long to wait for some action. The phoney war ended, Dunkirk happened and children began leaving the towns and cities again in droves.

Typically my stubborn mother dug in her heels and we stayed. One headlong rush from home, she said, was enough. We would Wait and See.

For several weeks chaos reigned supreme as the Luftwaffe became regular visitors. First along the South and East Anglian coastal airfields, then further and further inland until the whole of Southern England became a battleground.

Secure in my twelve year old perception of my own invulnerability, certain beyond all doubt that no bomb would ever fall from the skies on *my* head, it was exciting beyond my wildest dreams to have lessons frequently interrupted by air raid warnings. Even the chanting of French verbs became bearable when crouched under our desks, and an innocent "*pardonits ma, pork quare, Mademoiselle?*" delivered with an excruciating accent, a plethora of rolled R's and a great deal of spit – something that could normally be guaranteed to goad the French mistress into apoplectic fury – was rendered safe when she was lying prone on the floor beneath her table and gabbling Hail Mary's at the rate of knots. I slept on a bunk in a garden shelter, peed in a bucket and ate like a gypsy with my plate on my lap, blissfully happy and heedless at first of falling bombs.

* * * * *

But this particular freedom from routine came at a heavy price. As the weeks passed and the raids increased from one or two sorties a day to wave after wave of bombers droning overhead both day and night, the need for sleep became rather more important than the pleasures of interrupted lessons and meals eaten *al fresco*, although there were compensations. My brother and I collected shrapnel after each raid, vying with each other as to who could find the largest piece, and we didn't get to wash as often or as thoroughly as in pre-shelter days. Bathing and hair washing became less frequent as leaping from a tepid bath and racing to the shelter naked but for a towel was deemed by my mother to be both unseemly and unpleasant. But on the night the land mine fell on the nearby cricket ground and we lost every single window in the house she apparently decided that enough was enough. The sight of gaping window frames and torn curtains rendering bare our most intimate belongings to any passing stranger ruffled even her hitherto unshaken calm. Stepping purposefully over the shattered glass and splintered

14

wood she declared with magnificent understatement: 'Well, I can see no point in being uncomfortable indefinitely. Perhaps it is time we went up to Worcestershire to join your Aunt Emily and the boys. They seem to be happy enough since they evacuated there'

'You mean we're going to be evacuees?' I could scarcely believe my ears; I had been sulking for months because I hadn't been allowed to go with the first flood of children. I was desperate to be an evacuee – preferably an authentic one like those from the local school, with a label on my coat, a packet of sandwiches in greaseproof paper, and Pathé News filming my brave smile. My brother said it was a good job that I wasn't amongst the trainloads leaving the great Metropolis, as I should undoubtedly have been the one left sitting in some village hall when all the more attractive ones had been chosen. He was probably right; by then even my mother had given up the struggle to curl my hair into fetching ringlets and get me into dainty dresses.

Not that she gave up easily; for years she tortured my hair into rags every Saturday night in the vain hope that on Sunday morning I'd leap out of bed transformed into Shirley Temple. But despite her best efforts and a sleepless night (mine), all she achieved were a few depressing ringlets. By the time I departed to Sunday school my hair hung as usual about my face like a deeply depressing and unsavoury hank of brown yarn, while the dainty dress had been reduced to a limp rag. She tried hard, but without the raw material of dimples and an expression at least verging on the right side of malevolent she really had little on which to work.

She had it tough, my mother; in the nineteen-thirties, if your girl child didn't look like Shirley Temple and go to dancing classes, or at least have dimples and look cute as a bunny or pixie in the local pantomime, you put a brave face on it and suffered the tortures of the damned; or the pity of the neighbours, which was worse.

As I scrunched over broken glass to find my favourite books and the leery-eyed stuffed monkey my father had brought back from Singapore, I reflected that being an evacuee, even a boring no label no Pathé News one was better than nothing. It would be fun living near Aunt Emily and seeing my little cousins again.

* * * * *

Within a few days our furniture had been put into store, the shattered windows boarded up and at long last we became evacuees. Little did my mother guess as the train left Paddington station – also denuded of glass – to what new perils she was leading her darling children.

Although the train was quite crowded we had a carriage to ourselves. This was not by chance or good fortune: we *always* had one to ourselves and there was a very good reason for this, namely: the Idiot Children Game.

My brother was almost four years my senior and generally treated me either with silent contempt, or as a useful slave to fetch and carry for him, not that I ever did much of that unless threatened with torture. But on this occasion, although morose at having to leave behind his collection of shrapnel, his horrible school-friends, the girl at the tobacconists who was reputed to have the biggest breasts in the county, and with the added humiliation of actually being seen in public with me, he was still mischievous enough to call a truce and play our time-honoured Repel All Boarders game

The method was simple and the effect instantaneous. Any unwary traveller rash enough to approach our carriage would scuttle away like a startled mouse on sighting a hungry cat. After all, who in their right mind would choose to spend a long journey with the two leering and possibly homicidal child maniacs hanging out of the train window and drooling all down the door?

The only surprising thing about the whole business was that my mother, normally an eagle-eyed observer of her children's misdeeds, always remained entirely unaware of what was going on right under her nose. On this occasion she sat in the opposite corner of the carriage knitting another pair of long white socks in the most disgustingly smelly oily unwashed wool for my father, in blissful ignorance of the unfortunate effect her children were having on any would-be passenger foolish enough to approach our carriage.

* * * * *

By the time our journey ended we were all three tired, and in my case fractious. The train had travelled in fits and starts; there were several air raid alerts and each one meant the train stopped and we waited, usually on a nerve-wracking exposed piece of track, whilst Hurricane and Messerschmitt fought it out above our heads. Shrub Hill Station, when we finally reached it seven hours after our departure from Paddington, was dark and dirty with only a few feeble blue-shaded lamps to light our way. It took ages to find a porter and even longer for the porter to find a taxi driver willing to make the long journey to our final destination. The only one prepared to accept my mother's hefty bribe turned out to have the oldest and probably the least reliable cab north of the Watford Gap.

Half choked with exhaust fumes, jolting and swaying on broken springs, we came at last to the Green Dragon Inn on the very edge of a dark, brooding forest, to a crossroads where once they hanged thieves and highwaymen on a gibbet and left them to rot in their chains. At least that's what the cab driver told us as he unceremoniously dumped our bags on the roadway, stuffed his ill-gotten gains in his pocket and departed with an

Edgar Allan Po-ish sort of leer.

Tired, dirty and dishevelled we stood for a few moments in silence before our new home. 'Oh, my God!' my mother gave a nervous laugh and held my hand tightly, eyeing uncertainly the dark, faintly sinister building that crouched like a great beast preparing to spring from the surrounding trees and bushes. 'For this we left civilisation – just wait until I get hold of Emily tomorrow ... "quaint old country Inn," my foot!'

'Perhaps it's haunted?' I suggested hopefully. My brother kneed me in the back.

'If it is they'll soon skedaddle when they get a dekko at *you*!'

My mother boxed his ears, not for kneeing me in the back but for using slang. While he was busy rubbing his head and complaining, I dropped my case on his foot and watched with malicious pleasure as he hopped around in the middle of the road holding his foot in both hands and yelling.

My mother said 'Oh, my God!' again in a resigned sort of voice and picked up her case. 'Come along,' she said, 'before someone calls out the Home Guard...'

THE GREEN DRAGON

At the Green Dragon

Even when viewed in the kindly light of day the Green Dragon was not a thing of beauty. Just a flat-faced late Georgian pile with sagging windows and an unlovely collection of outhouses and barns, the whole surrounded by a riot of untrimmed bushes and four massive beeches towering above the crooked slate roof. But on that late August evening in 1940 it was, despite its imperfections, welcoming enough, as we dragged our suitcases into the warmth and light of the cosy parlour behind the spit 'n sawdust public bar and the only slightly more salubrious saloon.

We were to have the parlour to ourselves and there were three bedrooms under the eaves prepared for us: the largest was for my mother, it had an enormously high brass bedstead and a huge wardrobe with all sorts of unpleasant looking carvings on the doors; the two smaller rooms, with just space in each for a bed, a narrow glass fronted wardrobe and a night table were for my brother and me. He immediately commandeered the slightly larger one that had a big window overlooking the garden, leaving me the poky one with a window the size of a postage stamp and view of the road, but by then I was just too tired to care.

That night for the first time in many weeks I climbed into a soft, sweet-smelling bed and in long forgotten peace and quiet slept, and slept and slept...

* * * * *

I awoke to afternoon sunlight streaming through a tiny window and the sound of loud talk and raucous laughter. Scrambling across the billows and troughs of my feather bed I pushed aside the curtain to peer with sleepy eyes at the outside world.

Beneath the window the wooden sign of the Green Dragon swung to and fro, creaking gently in the breeze; on the road below a group of boys and girls were shoving and scrambling as they flipped marbles along in the dust. As they appeared to be speaking a foreign tongue I pushed wide the window, straining my ears to untangle the rapid exchange of words, but apart from one or two recognisable swear words I didn't understand a thing and gave up defeated.

They were what my mother would deem a Rough Crowd, the boys mainly shaven-headed (a necessary nit-avoidance tactic I discovered later). Despite the warmth of the sun they all wore jerseys, not very clean trousers and very large aggressive looking boots. The girls looked only slightly better in faded cotton frocks and knitted cardigans. Their hair, which sported a variety of ribbons, tape and in the odd case string, was mostly worn long. Nits it seemed were OK for girls.

Enthralled by all the rough language, punching, shoving and vociferous squabbling over the marbles, I watched from behind the curtains until they were out of sight, quite unaware then that I was about to journey into a hitherto unknown world of comradeship and adventure with these same children, the memory of which would stay with me all the days of my life, vivid and glowing as that first sun-drenched afternoon.

* * * * *

On arrival the previous evening we had all been grateful to accept a hot drink from our landlady before sinking into bed for that long and desperately needed sleep, and my awakening to the sounds of the village children beneath my window had left me in a strange kind of limbo. I snuggled back under the covers and tested my feelings about this alien place. What would it be like living in a pub? I was sure my mother had never been in such a place, let alone lived in one. The smell rising from the taproom beneath the floorboards was unfamiliar but strangely satisfying and rich; in retrospect perhaps the seeds of my adult fondness for country bars and ale were sown on that first morning at the Green Dragon.

Remembering our arrival the previous evening and the greeting from our landlord and his wife, I was overcome by a fit of the giggles, which I hastily stifled with a pillow in case my mother heard. In our house you could laugh as much as you liked, but not giggle; giggling, my mother said, set her teeth on edge, which seemed odd because you could giggle as much as you liked with my father – it was sniffing that put *his* teeth on edge.

Grown-ups, I had realised very early in life, were totally unpredictable and liable to be upset by the oddest things.

Mr and Mrs 'Arris (it was only later I discovered Harris had an aitch, but by then had been brainwashed by them both into not using it) were a bit like Laurel and Hardy. Mr, being small and thin and bewildered, resembled Little Stan with the addition of a drooping moustache. Mrs however was even larger and more rotund than Ollie; in fact she was simply HUGE: all red-faced and wobbly with a bosom that you could sit a teacup on.

She had hard-looking severely bobbed black hair, very small eyes in a very large face and her curves were held in check by the sort of apron worn under their shawls by the old women of the French Revolution, who sat around the guillotine waiting for aristocratic heads to hit the basket. I thought Mr 'Arris had kind eyes and was probably nice, but reserved judgement on Mrs 'Arris. Quite apart from the apron, her powerful arms reminded me of our Monday wash lady, Mrs Rawlins, who was almost as big and had hairy moles on her chin. She would mutter beneath her breath as she shoved my dresses through the wooden mangle as though she wished it were me she was flattening, which it probably was. I had nightmares about her for years. This was partly due to my father's observation at the tea table one day that if I ate any more bread and butter I would end up looking like Mrs Rawlins: a horrendous fate for a sensitive child to contemplate.

After my long sleep I was dying to relieve my bursting bladder, and remembering the instructions issued by Mrs 'Arris as I stumbled up the stairs the previous night, fished under the bed and discovered the most enormous chamber pot, heavily decorated with cabbage roses and trailing vines. On the inside was inscribed a verse of a Marie Lloyd song that began 'I sits amongst the cabbages and peas.'

Availing myself of the invitation then dabbling my fingers in the water jug and wiping them over my face, I dressed quickly and went downstairs in search of my brother. I found him seated at a large wooden table before the glowing range, shovelling bacon and eggs and potatoes down his throat as though he expected they might disappear at any moment from off his plate.

He paused only to wave a fork dripping with egg yolk. 'Hurry up, dozy, and get some of this food – this place is absolutely wizard – the bog's down the garden; it pongs like a million doggie doh-dahs and mum says to hold your breath as

22

much as you can! We all missed breakfast and lunch so Mum's making a cooked tea through there…' and he gestured to the open door at the far end of the room.

'Yuk!' I looked with loathing at his chomping jaws but, marvelling at the sight of *real* eggs, hurried through the doorway and found my mother in a vast cavern of a kitchen frying thick rashers of bacon over an even larger black-leaded range.

'Look!' she said, 'I may go mad with boredom here but we certainly won't starve!' She laughed and I stood for a moment staring at her because it seemed so long since I had seen her really laugh. 'Come here.' She held out her arms and gave me a hug. 'I know it all seems strange, but you mustn't worry; you'll soon get used to it.'

I was going to say I didn't mind at all and tell her about the children I'd watched from the window; then prudently held my peace. It was, I had discovered by trial and error, often more productive not to let adults know when you were content – sometimes it made them suspicious and you might miss out when any treat was in the offing.

* * * * *

The Forest worked its magic on us all. Reunited with her younger sister and away from the constant threat of air raids my mother became increasingly carefree and happy; allowing us a kind of freedom we had never known before.

Overnight a whole new world opened to us; we climbed trees, swooped down Furze Hill two-up on an ancient bicycle we'd discovered rusting in an outhouse; flung dried, and not so dried, cowpats in exciting battles and generally ran wild. The bicycle made for a particularly thrilling ride, as it had no brakes. Stopping at the finish of our rush down the hill could only be effected by riding onto the rough grass verge for the last thirty yards or so before the cross roads, then crashing along the final few feet in the ditch. It was painful on the knees and elbows but the excitement of the ride was well worth all the cuts and bruises. Once we nearly ran over the village policeman who gave us each a pretty hefty whack across the backs of our heads as a warning not to do it again. We didn't, of course, take the slightest notice; only made sure he was nowhere about on subsequent rides.

* * * * *

One morning shortly after our arrival my brother and I left my mother mastering the intricacies of bread-making and ventured beyond Furze Hill and the Green Dragon. Walking along the wide road that led towards Bewdley and about a quarter of a mile from the Inn we came upon the village store, a painted sign above the low door informing us the owner was a Miss Alice Wassdal who was licensed to sell Alcohol and Tobacco. By the look of it she sold everything else as well, from groceries and shoe laces to watering cans and tin bathtubs. Venturing inside we were faced with a long wooden counter at one end of which stood a large hand-operated bacon slicer, while at the opposite end was a kind of cage that turned out to be the Post Office.

Loitering before a stand of dusty postcards bearing views of Worcester Cathedral we watched as villagers came and went. Before serving any customer with a penny stamp or a postal order Miss Alice, as we discovered she was addressed, would carefully remove her wrap-around floral apron, snap on a pair of celluloid cuffs and enter the cage ready to conduct her official Post Office duties. When at the end of our first month in the village my mother went to cash her Naval Allowance there was terrible consternation when the Post Office didn't have enough money in the till. Naturally word got around that 'They lot at t' pub's a load o' girt rich boogers' and it took a long time to live down this unflattering and erroneous view of the Forrow family fortunes.

Miss Alice, we quickly discovered, was every child's dream of the perfect maiden aunt, and when she got to know us was forever slipping us handfuls of broken biscuits from the glass-topped tins lining the front of the counter. She was fascinated to discover that I knew most of the outdated Music Hall songs (one of my few accomplishments and one that drove my mother mad). When suitably bribed I was willing to stand on the counter to perform *I'm Burlington Bertie From Bow* or *My Old Man Said Follow The Van* while tears of laughter ran down Miss Alice's face and were wiped away with a corner of her overall. Once, oh, joy of joys, she gave Peter and me a whole penny bar of Nestlés chocolate each for an encore.

I rather suspected it was my brother's presence as much as my singing that brought forth these goodies; he was darkly handsome and just a touch too beautiful to be true; at almost sixteen he could already reduce old, and not so old ladies to pink-cheek slavery. My usual reaction to the winsome smile in his glossy brown spaniel eyes was to give him a good hack on the shins, but I dared not risk doing that when such toothsome handouts were on offer.

* * * * *

In those few weeks before school started, when we were forced to rely on each other for company, I began for the first time in my life to quite like my brother. Up until then the only thing we had ever previously shared without fighting was whooping cough when I was ten. I couldn't see why he always seemed to come first with my mother and hardly ever got told off. He seldom gave me a civil word and would proclaim *sotto voci* in restaurants that I could sit next to him but not opposite as my face put him off his food. At Christmas and Birthdays he received exciting presents, such as an air rifle, roller skates, a steam engine, while I had to write Thank You letters for dolls, sewing baskets, knitting and embroidery kits, all of which I viewed with contempt. It was all terribly unfair and I spent a great deal of time and energy trying to devise a method of killing him that would fool even Sherlock Holmes into discounting the possibility of foul play.

Only once did I come close to achieving my hearts desire when one rainy morning he slipped on the wet concrete of the garden path and knocked himself out. Quick as a flash I jumped on top and gave his head a few more hearty bangs on the concrete before fleeing to my bedroom to await with bated breath the discovery of his dead body. I can still remember my bewildered fury when I was called down to tea and discovered him as large as life, scoffing cream cakes and apparently none the worse for wear.

Before the war when we had our Saturday pocket money I spent mine on a collection of lead gnomes from Woolworth's for my garden rockery, and he spent his on miniature cacti for his bedroom windowsill. Once, in a fit of rage because I'd used his roller skates and lost the key, he riddled all my gnomes with airgun pellets and I retaliated by fastening the elastic on the ball of the Tennis Come-Back to the light flex in his bedroom, then perching on the far window sill pulled back the elastic to its full length before letting go the ball. With whoops of triumph I sent fifteen cacti spinning out of the open window and crashing onto the paved terrace below. It was my finest hour.

But now of necessity we had increasingly to rely upon each other for company and for a time at least I put my plans for fratricide to one side.

Our cousins were very much younger, the eldest only seven years old, his brother just a baby, so as companions they were pretty useless. I was a little shy of making friendly overtures to the few children we saw – and there were only a few. Miss Alice explained that this was because 'It's 'arvest, m'dears an' they all be out wurking in the fields.' This form of slavery apparently included most of the evacuees. Billeted on farms and smallholdings, they were in the main shamelessly exploited by their temporary foster parents alongside their own children as unpaid labour. Although I doubt that a skinny twelve year old was my brother's idea of a perfect companion, in this unfamiliar environment we closed ranks and grew, for a time, closer together.

* * * * *

However, all too soon it was September and school loomed over these halcyon days like a large black cloud. My brother was easily settled and departed to the Grammar School in nearby Bewdley, a distance of some five miles, which he covered each day on a new – *new*, mark you – bicycle, with drop handlebars, Sturmey-Archer gears and dynamo lamps. His superiority and my sense of grievance returned with a vengeance and it was another five years at least before we could begin to appreciate each other again and become friends.

Once he was no longer around, I was left alone to kick my heels with nothing much to do but entice the barn cats into the pub and drive Mrs 'Arris wild. She hated cats and only tolerated them in the barns because they kept the rat population within reasonable bounds, so I was not one of her favourite people. She would stomp about, all her chins a-quiver, muttering darkly about 'Some little madam needin' 'er backside tarned good an' proper' and urging my mother to send me to the village school.

Now since the age of five I had attended a small private school in Woodford presided over by Miss Lee (aka Mr Brocklehurst), a formidable lady of extreme and terrifying gentility. My mother was naturally loath to risk my expensively acquired veneer of ladylike behaviour being dispelled by the village school, but as my aunt pointed out, so far her small son had survived it unharmed (much *she* knew) and there really was no alternative. Eventually my mother was forced to capitulate, much to my carefully concealed joy. The boys and girls, who had begun to pass the Green Dragon on their way to school engrossed in pushing each other into ditches and behaving generally with a delightful lack of restraint, were to my eyes ideal companions. As I set off with my mother one crisp September morning I had a jolly good idea that this school was likely to be a far cry from Miss Lee's and its well-brought-up young ladies.

I was not to be disappointed.

THE VILLAGE SCHOOL

"Feed My Lambs"

The Village School had a deceptively benign appearance, being a typical Victorian building with pleasing gables and large high-placed windows. From the heavy wooden gate a broad gravelled pathway led through grass to the front of the building; behind it an asphalt playground could be glimpsed through the oak trees that flanked either side. It looked like a picture postcard of the perfect rural school. Lending weight to this idyllic impression, the inscription FEED MY LAMBS was carved into a long beam beneath the main gable. Passing this exhortation we walked into the main hall and were conducted by a buxom but runny-nosed maiden to where the teaching staff, comprising Mr Mole, Mrs Mole and Mrs Brown, stood in a row by the far doors.

We approached them, me wide-eyed with wonder and stifling an overwhelming desire to giggle, my mother blenching visibly.

29

Mr Mole was tall and gaunt with cadaverous cheeks and bushy eyebrows that met in the middle. His lady wife (dusted down and fetched back into the classroom when the younger teachers left to do war work) was a fat, squat female bearing a remarkable, one might say uncanny, resemblance to the Shepherd drawings of Toad of Toad Hall in drag. Mrs Brown (also dusted down, etc) appeared to my young eyes as an aged crone; she was perhaps somewhat past fifty, had a fine moustache and was, on closer acquaintance, deaf as the proverbial post.

Culture shock would I suppose be the modern term to describe my feelings. God only knew what might have described my mother's. Certainly *I* had never seen such an ugly trio outside of a fairground and they looked like no other teachers I had ever met, even although weird teachers were nothing new to me.

At Miss Lee's, eccentricity went with the brown knitted skirts and hair in a bun, apart from Miss Richards who had *her* hair cropped like a man, wore shirts and ties and was known to one and all as Neuter. She could often be deflected from grinding vast amounts of Shakespeare into our already over-burdened brains by being side-tracked into reciting 'The Highwayman' or, even better, 'Ode to a Bulldog'. Edged on by an admiring audience Neuter would fling herself into The Highwayman with gusto. When she got to,

> *'They shot him down on the highway;*
> *Down like a dog on the highway,*
> *And he lay in his blood on the highway,*
> *A dark red stain at his throat'*

we would all throw ourselves weeping and howling onto our desks. Sir John Squire's poem from the Great War that begins:

> *'We shan't see Willy any more, Maimie,*
> *He won't be coming home any more'*

and ends with the heartrending,

> *'So I must sit, not speaking on the sofa,*
> *While you lie asleep on the floor;*
> *For he's suffered a thing that dogs couldn't dream of,*
> *And he won't be coming home any more,'*

she would read in a deeply tragic baritone which was sufficient to bring forth tears enough to wash a fair sized floor.

With a bit of luck all these emotional outpourings could be prolonged until the bell went for break.

* * * * *

Duly registered as a member (number thirty eight) of Miss Brown's class, and after the departure of my bemused and distinctly apprehensive looking mother, I was returned to the main hall to experience the eye-opening, mind-blowing initiation into Morning Prayers as conducted by the fearsome cadaverous Mr Mole.

Into the large central hall, which doubled as the top classroom, with its tiers of iron-bound desks and benches rising step by step in a semicircle before the high master's desk (placed conveniently for *his* warmth beside the large Tortoise stove), Mr Mole's charges crowded elbow to elbow. A packed mass of some hundred or more children aged five to fourteen were whispering, pinching and shoving each other and shuffling their hobnailed boots; the noise and smells reminiscent of a badly run zoo. Hacking coughs rent the air while spitting, at the floor and the heads of those in front, appeared to be the order of the day and elbows came into their own as offensive weapons used to secure a modicum of personal space in this heaving throng.

A sudden yell of 'QUIET!' from Mr Mole as he swept

through the door produced instant silence from all and a puddle on the floor from a small ginger-haired child on my left. Mr Mole then began rattling off the Lord's Prayer at great speed with all of us gabbling away two phrases behind him until he got to Forgive Us Our Trespasses, when he stopped suddenly to rend the air with another yell.

'You, boy – you – picking your nose! Filthy little booger!' A hefty prayer book flew through the air, missing the nose-picker and felling an innocent bystander while the nose-picker took off over the desks at speed hotly pursued by Mole clutching a stick and swearing like a Billingsgate fish porter.

I was enthralled; nothing like this ever happened with Miss Lee leading morning prayers. After a couple of circuits of hare and hounds over the desks with all and sundry dodging the nose-picker's boots and Mole's stick, the luckless boy was collared, thumped and dumped in the corner, and led by the headmaster we all resumed the Lord's Prayer where he had left off. This, I subsequently discovered, was par for the course and morning prayers as conducted by the volatile Mr Mole continued to offer all the thrills and spills of an out of control roller-coaster.

Once settled into Mrs Brown's classroom I quickly grasped the bucolic 'yes'm' and 'no'm' which were apparently *de riguer* when speaking to a female teacher, and by the end of the morning had advanced well into the game played by the entire class on poor Miss Brown. This consisted of swallowing vast amounts of air in order to conduct all conversations on the longest possible rolling belch, whilst the less able contented themselves with a discreet *Aaaarchbishop* or *Eeeaaarrrrwig*. Connoisseurs of the art could manage a couple of sentences on one single belch whilst remaining poker faced amid the titters and occasional outright guffaws of their peers. Serene in the cocoon of her deafness, largely oblivious of the uproar around her Mrs Brown carried on with the Wars of the Roses; pausing only to smack the heads of the most blatant and uncontrolled gigglers, of whom I was one.

* * * * *

Mid-morning break was the signal for the kind of mayhem usually associated with a Saturday morning cinema showing of the Keystone Cops; first a mad concerted rush for the odoriferous brick built privies in the centre of the playground – girls on one side, boys on the other, with quite a few not actually making it to the buckets – then small boys with outstretched arms raced screaming around the playground being Spitfires, while bigger boys roared back and forth playing British Bulldog. Fighting for space in the midst of this chaos, with dresses tucked into knickers and skipping ropes flailing, determined females jumped up and down chanting *'My Mother said that I never should, play with the gypsies in the wood'* which was all very nice and girly until on closer examination one noticed that with a few adroit flicks of the rope quite a lot of passing Bulldogs and Spitfires were sent nose-diving onto the gritty asphalt.

Content on this first day to be a spectator, I stood in the shelter of a buttress letting the yelling throng eddy around me until Mr Mole, cane held aloft as though about to lead a cavalry charge appeared like a manic Jack-in-the Box from a door a few feet away and screamed 'LINES!' at the full pitch of his lungs.

Instantly, as at morning prayers, silence fell. Girls hauled their dresses out of their knickers and raced with Bulldogs and Spitfires to form two rigid lines before the doors, one of boys, one of girls, and I scuttled to join them, almost falling over Mole's feet in my haste.

The lines tensed, like greyhounds waiting for the trap to spring, as Mole inflated his chest almost to bursting point and his face turned purple; 'MARCH!' he roared, whereupon everyone marched at once and quite a few got jammed in the doors. Wielding his cane Mole then leaped upon the hapless bundle stuck in the doorway and they shot through into the corridor like corks from a bottle.

After all this, Mrs Brown's classroom appeared as a haven of peace, rolling belches not withstanding.

At lunchtime we were allowed out onto the field at the side of the school to eat our sandwiches. I found my little cousin, who at morning break had been in the little one's playground, and as we shared our sandwiches I began to make friends amongst the other children.

But with the coming of afternoon school, Toad of Toad Hall arrived in place of Mrs Brown and proved to be no fun at all. For a start she smacked heads much harder and more frequently and there was nothing wrong with *her* hearing, quite the reverse. Being totally useless at either of her specialised subjects which were knitting and needlework, I longed more than ever to be a boy. Although no sane child would have actually chosen to do woodwork with Mr Mole, I felt anything would have been preferable to an afternoon spent closeted with his lady wife. My head was soon ringing from frequent contact with her horny toad palm as I laboured to knit a pink vest for a refugee child. God help the unfortunate who eventually got it for no one could have been *that* hard up. The first two inches had more holes in it than a shot blasted pigeon and in the following weeks it became increasingly holed, murky and unsavoury in my sweaty and grubby hands. Never had the going-home bell sounded so sweet to my ears.

* * * * *

At long last my first day at the Village School was at an end and I was free to trudge the long dusty road back to the Green Dragon. I've often wondered what made me relatively immune

34

to the atmosphere of verbal and physical violence; most of my fellow evacuees were. Perhaps as a survivor of Miss Lee's Academy I had a head start, because for all her gentility that lady possessed a tongue dipped in vitriol and wielded a ruler with as much aim and enthusiasm as one of Cromwell's serial iconoclasts whacking hell out of a papist. To this day I hold firmly to the belief that she was the unacknowledged inventor of plastic: how else could she have been the possessor of a foot and a half of *flexible* ruler? It most certainly wasn't made of wood, Neuter had one of those and it made little impression on grubby ink stained palms. Miss Lee's ruler was an entirely different kettle of fish.

She taught us Arithmetic, Geometry and Algebra and woe betide the child who didn't pay attention or got it wrong. As I was guilty on both counts I became remarkably – one might almost say exceptionally – well acquainted with Miss Lee's flexible ruler.

It was a waste of time to run home at the end of the day with stinging palms and expect sympathy. My mother would invariably halt my complaints of brutality with the tart obs-ervation that I must have done something to deserve it. Consequently I learned to keep the results of my misdeeds under wraps and seldom allowed them to cross the line between home and school, so on my return to the Green Dragon that afternoon I breathed not a word to my mother about all the clouts from the teachers, or the appalling language both from Mr Mole and my peers. I wasn't stupid; one whiff of what really went on behind that exhortation to 'Feed My Lambs' and I reckoned I would have been whisked out of there and sent to a convent – a threat which was frequently held over my head. Though why a convent I have no idea, as my mother disapproved strongly of subservient women and thought any female who voluntarily spent half her life on her knees must be certifiably insane.

The next day she was amazed at my anxiety to get to school

and I overheard her telling Mrs 'Arris that I seemed so happy and content that I had obviously made a very good start at my new school.

How right she was.

Games and Diversions

I suppose it was inevitable that the nose picker and I should become bosom friends. His name was Georgie Little, and despite the difference in sex and upbringing, deep down we were two of a kind: determined to outwit authority, contemptuous of grown-ups in general and schoolteachers in particular.

We were drawn together that first day in the classroom when, during a lull in the belching contests, I heard him utter a word of such electrifying wickedness that I snorted aloud with laughter and earned myself a thump in the back from Mrs Brown that made my teeth rattle.

Our eyes met: one of his closed in a wink and before my startled gaze he raised two derisive fingers at Mrs Brown's departing rear. Consumed with a mixture of shock and delight I stared with open mouthed admiration at his snub-nosed face with its dusting of dirt and freckles, beneath an untidy thatch of tow coloured hair, and knew I had found both ally and friend.

When I left the Green Dragon early next morning he was waiting for me. 'Thought cher might not know the cut through the forest,' he said by way of greeting and explanation, and that was that. Without another word spoken we set off together through the forest, along the narrow winding path beaten through the ferns and brambles by generations of children in the erroneous belief that it shortened the journey to school. Walking it some fifty years later I realised that it was in fact at least a quarter of a mile longer than making the journey by the road; but what did that matter? On the road there was always someone watching and ready to stop you having fun; in the forest we could be Robin Hood and Little John or The Lone Ranger and Tonto, or even Dick Barton and Snowy.

Of course Georgie was what my mother would call a Bad Influence, which was exactly what made him so attractive. Once our friendship was established and each had implicit trust in the other, it wasn't long before I was keeping Mrs 'Arris busy chatting in the kitchen whilst Georgie nipped into the bar and helped himself to a paper packet of five Woodbines from beneath the counter. Repairing to the forest with our booty we would sit on our favourite fallen tree and puff away like experts. Once we took my little cousin but he was sick and nearly gave the game away. Occasionally my brother joined us on a Saturday and showed off by smoking De Reske Minors but we weren't jealous; stolen fruits are always sweeter. We tried hard to teach him the belching game but he never did master it; he was, I told him with malicious glee, too old to adapt – a matter I savoured to the full as I was so very seldom able to either feel or be superior to him in any other respect.

The best thing about those walks to school while the mornings were still light enough for us to see our way were the games we played. All through September and October almost everyone had a hoop of some kind: mostly small metal cart or bicycle rims, or a few of the proper wooden ones Miss Alice sold in the shop. Racing these along the narrow path at speed meant frequent collisions and not a few fights. Spinning tops were even more excitingly dangerous; lashed along in the dirt with leather thongs they could be made to rebound off trees or whizzed after a fleeing enemy. Marbles, always the favourites, were fiercely battled for in running games that not infrequently led to fists and boots flying over some precious Blood Alley or Alley Taw.

But the best game of all in those early weeks was conkers, and the finest Horse Chestnut tree for miles was at Allen's farm, just where the forest path joined the road. Its massive branches overhung a high wall, allowing the green husks to shower down across the roadway, inviting all who passed by to plunder the gloriously large shiny fruits.

However, there was a problem, or rather two problems, for Allen's farm was home to a pair of evacuee brothers. The younger, for some mysterious reason named 'Dollops', was notorious in the village as the new evacuee who on arrival had stood in the road hurling insults and abuse at every child who passed by. This had surprised everyone, as Dollops was a small bespectacled child with refined vowels, not at all the type to go looking for trouble in quite so public a fashion. He never seemed to learn from his mistakes so spent a great deal of time with Elastoplasts holding his spectacles together.

Perched high on the wall, he and his brother defended the conkers with a ferocity that kept most at bay, any approach to the tree being met by a volley of stones, dried cowpats, mud balls and half bricks. The older brother had a powerful over-arm action that marked him as a possible future Test cricketer, a promise, alas, never to be fulfilled. I know, because sixteen years later we were married with Dollops as our best man…but that is another story.

Even so, I've never actually forgiven either of them for ruining the conker season for the rest of us.

The weather began to grow colder. Mornings were crisp and nights decidedly chilly. By the end of October we were setting off for school in the dark, huddling in tight groups, even the bravest glad to keep close for comfort.

However, before we were allowed to leave the Green Dragon my brother and I had the horrible task of cleaning the glass chimneys and trimming the wicks of the oil lamps. There was no electricity in the village and the two big brass lamps in our sitting room and the three smaller ones with which we lit our way to bed each night had to be cleaned daily. We complained bitterly but to no avail. Every morning before school, swathed in a couple of Mrs 'Arris's voluminous wrap-around aprons, which wrapped-around me about five times so that I ended up looking like a bundle of badly tied washing, we slaved by the light of candles; first trimming the sooty wicks with nail scissors then washing the chimneys in soapy water before drying and polishing them until they shone to my mother's exacting standards. Afterwards, the smell of paraffin lingered on clothes and skin for hours and just the faintest whiff of it, even after so long, still recalls vividly to my mind those cold bleak mornings spent around the kitchen table at the Green Dragon.

The highlight of the week, though, was bathing in the tin bungalow bath before the kitchen range. It was bliss and we always fought over who would work the pump at the scullery sink to bring up the water to fill the huge copper basin set in a round of bricks over a glowing fire. Once the water was hot it was ladled out with a wooden-handled bailer and transported by bucket to the bath, which was surrounded by a wooden clothes-horse draped in towels; this contraption affording some privacy for the occupant and a token wind break to the cold draughts that whistled beneath the outer scullery door.

We were the lucky ones; most of the villagers had their pumps out in the yard, so carting the heavy buckets to and from their coppers was not a popular activity. Georgie boasted that *his* family only had a bath once a month in the winter and all in the same water but, as my mother observed, with ten in the family that was hardly surprising.

When the evil moment could no longer be delayed Mrs Little would equip her large brood with bowls and buckets and the entire family, muffled in hats coats, scarves and stout boots formed a human chain from the well to the scullery door. Once the water was heated and the bath ready the smallest went in first to emerge pink as a shrimp, then the next in line and so on through the family, finishing with father who might or might not immerse briefly in the by now tepid and murky water. Quite often, Georgie said, he went to the pub instead.

* * * * *

It grew too cold for sitting around on our fallen tree in the forest, so for a while Mrs 'Arris' Woodbines remained on the shelf under the counter while we prowled the various outhouses at the Green Dragon in search of sanctuary. Unfortunately we were invariably turned out by Mr 'Arris, who liked to enjoy a quiet pipe in solitude. We guessed it was his way of escaping from Mrs 'Arris and the myriad of tasks she would drive him to perform every time he showed his nose in the pub.

We were beginning to think we should have to take to playing Snakes and Ladders in the parlour, until one morning fate delivered into our grubby hands salvation in the unwitting persons of Mavis and Mickey Harper....

THE DES. RES.

The Des. Res.

It was unusual by November 1940 to see any new faces in school. However, on a bitter morning towards the end of that month, when we had trudged to school bundled into thick woollen coats, scarves and balaclava helmets for our daily dose of Mole Mania, there they were: pink and scrubbed and innocent as two little sacrificial pigs.

'Reckon they'm got any sweets?' enquired Georgie in a practised whisper, eyeing up the new arrivals. 'Dunno,' I muttered from the side of my mouth, 'but I wouldn't mind betting their sandwiches are better than ours!'

'QUIET!' yelled Mole, and this time Georgie got the prayer book, smack on the side of his head. I saw the boy staring in horror at this introduction to Mole's disciplinary methods. He looked as though he was about to flee in terror until I caught his eye, smiled winsomely and gave him a reassuring wink. His lower lip trembled then hesitantly he returned my smile with one of beguiling sweetness.

Under cover of the desk Georgie and I shook hands. 'You'm got 'im!' he breathed. 'Wait fer playtime an' I'll sort 'is sister!'

At morning break we two corralled the new arrivals in a corner of the playground and went to work.

They were touchingly pleased to be protected by us from the screaming hoards in the playground and willingly parted with a generous share of their Liquorice Allsorts and a promise to swap their lunchtime sandwiches (cold ham and tomato) with ours (jam from Georgie; cheese and viciously sour pickle from me).

* * * * *

Mavis and Mickey we discovered were not *real* evacuees; they hadn't fled any areas of saturation bombing; had come in fact from a sleepy Cornish village. Their father had been posted to an RAF camp near Cleobury Mortimer, and in order for him to come home on his short leaves Mrs Harper had rented the old gamekeeper's cottage on Furze hill, a stone's throw from the Green Dragon.

'Ar, Keep'r's Co'ige,' Georgie nodded sagely at Mavis and Mickey as we four huddled into a corner of the playground, peeling each layer from the Allsorts and sucking them one at a time to make them last as long as possible. 'You'm got a noice ol' pig sty there, n't chur?'

The Harper's looked puzzled. Mavis asked, 'Have we?'

'Yur – make a smashin' den. Luv'ly an' warm.'

'And a long way from the house...' I did my smiling bit again at Mickey and he blushed. At ten years old he was a pushover. 'Haven't you noticed? It's right down at the end of the orchard in amongst the blackberry bushes.'

'Yeah,' Georgie was elaborately casual. 'There n't been no pigs there fer years. We could help you'm turn it into a proper den; clean it up a bit; get some ol' carpet n' stuff.'

'Wouldn't that be lovely, Mickey?' Mavis' smile was radiant. 'We could take our teddies and dollies there and have tea parties.'

'Yeah!' said Georgie.

'What fun that would be!' I said.

Georgie and I exchanged looks, marvelling that it had taken such a short time to cement this promising friendship, and with such ease. The gang of two looked set fair to become the gang of four and our future winter out-of-school activities started to look a great deal more promising than before.

* * * * *

'I met a charming woman in the shop this morning,' said my mother as we were having supper that evening, 'Mrs Harper; she has two children, a boy and girl just starting at the school. When I explained that we were quite close neighbours she said she hoped you would be great friends.'

'How sweet!' my brother kicked me under the table. 'Isn't that just what you need – some *nice* little friends?'

I didn't deign to answer this, just stuck out my tongue and narrowed my eyes at him when my mother's back was turned. Wracking my brain for a suitable comeback, one which would cause him the maximum amount of trouble while leaving me in the clear, I waited until my mother had left the room to fetch more milk from the outhouse, then stared hard at the door of the corner cupboard for a few moments. 'Gosh!' I exclaimed excitedly. 'Something moved! I think that mouse is back again!'

'Wow!' he jumped up and shot around the table, 'where?'

While his head was well inside the cupboard I whipped the salt cellar from the dresser and emptied it into his tea before popping it back on the dresser. 'Too slow,' I advised smugly, 'you've missed it!'

He was half way through his tea before he reached the contents of the saltcellar. While he spat tea and salt all over the tablecloth and had his ears boxed by my mother, I drank my tea nicely and smiled at him over my cup.

Revenge is sweet.

* * * * *

Mavis and Mickey were hard going. They were extremely prim and incredibly dim; however, after a few weeks at the village school and a good deal of extra tuition from Georgie and me, they acquired a few rough edges and became almost tolerable. Unfortunately their mother, an elegant Wallis Simpson look-alike, was far from enamoured of her 'Two Chicks' as she called them, associating with us, complaining to their father when he came home on leave that we must be the ones responsible for their use of bad language. The next time we called for the two chicks the Wing Commander took us aside and, not without a twinkle in his eye, pointed out that while he personally had no objection to the Anglo-Saxon vernacular, four-letter words tended to upset his wife. Accordingly, he'd be most awfully pleased if in future we would keep them under wraps when his children were around.

As he was handsome and had medal ribbons which meant he was a hero, we readily acceded to this request but were furious with the chicks for dropping us in it. While every child in the village, whether young or old, swore like the proverbial trooper, only Mickey and Mavis were apparently thick enough to air the more depraved items in their new vocabulary in front of an adult. Still, there was the pigsty to consider and for the use of that we were prepared to overlook their temporary entry in our black books and forgive, if not forget.

* * * * *

We begged, borrowed (and in Georgie's case, stole) what we needed to turn the double pigsty into a cosy Des. Res. A couple of old rag rugs generously donated by my aunt's landlady covered the brick floors; a packing case from the Harper's cottage with a chenille cloth (filched from their mother's linen cupboard) over it made a table. Two milking stools from the 'Arris's barn and a couple of rickety unmatched chairs rescued from a neighbour's bonfire completed the furnishing. But the crowning glory and our proudest possession was an ancient wind-up gramophone complete with a large metal horn. This splendid object had been 'found' by Georgie in the Vicar's shed, together with a tin of slightly rusted needles, and duly installed in a corner of our den; the fact that he could only 'find' two records mattered not at all. One record was of an apparently certifiable lunatic singing *The Laughing Policeman* and a ditty entitled *Ain't It Grand To Be Blooming Well Dead* – a strange choice one felt for a Vicar – the other bursting forth into the full glory of Richard Tauber, giving *You are My Hearts Delight* and *Only a Rose* everything he'd got.

These we played over and over, until only a practised ear could discern the words through the hiss and crackle of their worn grooves.

* * * * *

It was my idea to create a fireplace with some bricks we found abandoned in the undergrowth. Jammed together into a six-inch-high square, they made a secure base for an old galvanised bucket with holes punched in its side. Wedged firmly into the bricks this made a perfect fire basket and all the wood needed to fuel a fire was to be found lying around the forest. A couple of tiles poked out of the roof got rid of most of the smoke, and when Georgie turned up one Saturday morning with a drain cover to balance on top of the bucket – Hey Presto! We had a cooker. It then needed only the acquisition of a frying pan (again, courtesy of the vicar's shed) and a small saucepan begged from Miss Alice for us to be in the business of home cooking in a big way. Bread, bacon and sausages disappeared from larders, and as winter advanced many happy hours were spent crouched over the fire bucket as we acquired extra meals and chilblains in about equal measure.

We also had a lot of stomach problems that winter. With hindsight I blame the drain cover. Georgie had pinched it from a farmyard soak-away and I'd lay evens that at the time he'd given it only a cursory rinse under the yard pump before using it as a grid on which to bake our potatoes.

Despite the chilblains and frequent attacks of what my father would have called the Bombay Trots, as the weather worsened we were glad to huddle over our fire and fill our stomachs with the extra food. In 1940 it was a hard winter across the country and in the villages it snowed and froze then snowed and froze again, day after day, until the tree branches snapped like matchwood and the road out of our own small hamlet became impassable by car or cart.

School was cancelled and daily we battled up Furze Hill to the den to cook and talk and squabble over games of draughts or Ludo. No one came near to disturb us and as Christmas approached we spent hours at our packing-case table colouring Christmas cards and embellishing them with bits of wool and the contents of little packets of rather dull metallic particles which in wartime passed for glitter.

It was a fairly Spartan Christmas all round. Snowbound as we were, those presents we hadn't made had to be purchased from Miss Alice's shop, which wasn't exactly bursting with up-to-the-minute gifts. But I was delighted with the contents of my own Christmas stocking. There was a new red and yellow Yo-Yo, a copy of Kenneth Graeme's *Dream Days* my mother had found at the Church Bazaar and a paint box with the colours in tubes instead of the usual hard blocks. There were cobnuts and raisins and an apple right down at the toe – my only disappointment, the lack of chocolate and the traditional tangerine.

But with almost every household keeping a pig or two there was no shortage of pork, and on Christmas day we had a wonderful festive meal with my aunt and cousins. They were billeted in a large house about a quarter of a mile from the Green Dragon, with plenty of room to play games and a dining table big enough to seat all of us, including the elderly couple who owned the house, for a very jolly dinner.

It was all a huge improvement on Christmas at home; there I would have had to endure a whole round of parties, including my own. I loathed the whole business of dressing up: shivering in the party dress made of georgette or some other equally scratch-making material; my sturdy Start-rites replaced by patent leather pumps, and a velvet (it had to be velvet) cloak worn in place of my warm woollen overcoat. With a floppy pink bow in the hair and a lace-trimmed hanky tucked into the knickers pocket, I would be deemed properly equipped to face the sickly food and the unspeakable agony of Party Games; the horror of Postman's knock with Archie Hamilton pressing wet kisses on my shrinking cheek, Pass the Parcel, always won by the most odious child in the room, Squeak-Piggy-Squeak, where one frequently ended up on the lap of a visiting hairy uncle who just loved playing with the children – and *that* would be more than his life was worth now.

After an hour of such torture I generally told my hostess that I felt sick and could I please go home? If she had already been unwise enough to offer me a plate of pink blancmange I'd probably have already been sick and was hung over the lavatory basin with a cold wet flannel for company while she frantically telephoned my mother to come and take me away.

All in all, a Worcestershire Christmas was a far more satisfactory affair; no party games were played *here*. We built gigantic snowmen, tobogganed down Furze Hill, and made snowballs until our hands froze inside our woollen gloves. Falling bombs and sleepless nights were now a far off bad dream and the magic of the forest, it seemed, would go on for ever.

With the New Year came a partial thaw. My mother was anxious to shop and my brother itching to spend his Christmas money, so we left on the one-bus-a-day to Kidderminster. This turned out to be something of a memorable journey as the roads still had all the charm of an eccentrically designed skating rink and the ancient driver swore all the way there and back.

But it was a wonderful day. I came home with a new knitted pixie hood, scarf and gloves and the nearest thing to a pair of boots that my mother would allow, and, by dint of a good deal of cajoling, one of the proper hairy hard-as-iron jerseys as worn by the village children. At last, I thought as I watched it parcelled in several-times-used brown paper, I would truly belong. The dialect I'd mastered without a problem, but the jerseys my mother knitted me had continued to mark me out as a vaccy. I was already burdened with not one, but *two* French names and this was handicap enough without the extra burden of brightly coloured jerseys with white Peter Pan collars.

My brother had spent all his money on a steam engine, a splendid affair of shining brass bolted to a polished wooden base which, when fuelled by Methylated spirit, was destined to run his latest Meccano creation. This was a towering structure which, so far as I could see, had no use and no point other than that its wheels could be made to go around with the right amount of power to drive them.

On our return he rushed up to his bedroom to test his new acquisition, only allowing me through the door to provide an admiring audience of one. Ceremoniously he cleared the windowsill and setting the engine tenderly down beside the Meccano began what I privately condemned as a general song and dance about very little. After much careful measuring of the methylated spirit, the meticulous adjustment of valves and priming and pumping of levers, the spirit was ignited, the fire door closed, and we sat back with bated breath to watch the wheels go around.

They went around all right: faster and faster until the whole structure began to shake and the odd screw came loose and hit the walls with a resounding crack. While I was bouncing on the bed and yelling with excitement my brother bent to make another adjustment to his beloved engine and received an accidental, well, *almost* accidental kick on his behind from my flailing legs that sent him cannoning head first into the whole structure. The Meccano crashed to the floor; the steam engine gave a despairing shriek and flames shot up the curtains.

My screams – as much of delight as terror – and my brother's howls of fury were deafening. The uproar brought Mrs 'Arris puffing up the stairs, her yells on catching sight of the conflagration surpassing anything that we could manage.

''Elp! 'EEEPL! Fire! 'elp!'

It was better than watching Charlie Chaplin at the Saturday

fleapit as Mr 'Arris, responding magnificently to her cries and showing hidden talent as an Olympic sprinter, tore up the stairs and heaved the fire bucket of freezing water across the room in the general direction of the conflagration. Unfortunately only a small amount reached the curtains, the rest being discharged fair and square over the bed and Mrs 'Arris, who had by then flung herself with outstretched arms between the fire and the patchwork quilt frequently referred to in capital letters as the Family Hairloom.

What followed was rather like one of those old Punch cartoons captioned 'Collapse of Stout Party', as Mrs 'Arris lay on the bed hyperventilating and clutching her bosom while Mr 'Arris stood at the door looking bewildered and clutching his empty bucket.

Still hurling insults and several interesting curses new even to me, my brother put out the flames with the contents of his water jug then started hitting me with it. I wasn't having that and retaliated with the remains of the Meccano so that by the time our mother arrived on the scene both of us were at it hammer and tongs and hell bent on killing each other.

Now mother had been a powerful swimmer and tennis player in her time, and we certainly felt the benefit of her strong right arm as, with the aid of a particularly long strut of the Meccano, she very quickly – and painfully – restored order. She calmed Mrs 'Arris, brought Mr 'Arris out of his catatonic trance then despatched us, bawling loudly, to the parlour where we proceeded to kick and hurl insults at each other, only ceasing when she reappeared and gave us the telling-off of a lifetime and another basting with the Meccano. As if all this wasn't enough, we then had to grovel to Mrs 'Arris *and* cough up the cash out of our pocket money for new curtains.

Our New Year may have started with a bang, but the reverberations were felt for several pocket-money-less weeks until we had discharged our debt; I of course was number one culprit for having caused the disaster and was barred, practically on pain of death, from even going *near* my brother's room ever again.

Next morning in the sty I recounted my woes.

'Doan' you worry about a piddlin' li'le steam engine,' comforted Georgie. 'That ain't nuthin' ter get upset about. S'only a toy, innit?'

'You'd have been bloody upset if you'd got hit with the Meccano!' I hoisted my skirt and clawed up my knickers leg to show my battle scars. Mavis squealed and even Georgie was impressed. Peering hard he said, 'Blimey! You'm c'n even see the 'oles!'

Only slightly mollified, I pulled my skirt down over my knees and glowered into the fire. 'One day,' I vowed through gritted teeth, 'one day I'll buy my *own* steam engine – a bloody great one – big enough to blow up the whole bloody pub!'

'Yeah,' Georgie grinned widely, 'but we'll get all the fags out the bar first, eh?'

Arrivals and Departures

There was one very important someone missing in my life at this time: my father. We had been used to his long absences ever since I could remember; serving on a New Zealand cruise liner he was often at sea for several months at the time and seldom home for Christmas. But by February 1941 he had been absent for seventeen months. In Hong Kong when war was declared, his ship had been requisitioned by the Navy, turned into an armed merchant cruiser and despatched to convoy duties in the Atlantic.

I don't think a single day passed without my thinking about him and wishing hopeless wishes for his return. I would mutter magic incantations to bring him home and play silent games in my head: if I could count backwards from a hundred without hesitating or making a mistake, or say the whole of the multiplication tables up to twelve before I'd climbed from the Green Dragon to the top of Furze Hill, he would come back. One morning I would wake up and find him there.

The possibility that he may never come back was ever present but pushed far into the deep recesses of my mind, too terrible to be acknowledged. Every Saturday evening we wrote letters without knowing when, or even if, they would ever reach him. Weeks would go by without reply then several of the familiar thin blue envelopes would arrive together. They were guarded, loving letters with no hint of where he was or what he was enduring. By the time we moved to Worcestershire he had been transferred to a frigate and still on convoy duties. As the shipping losses mounted my mother would take herself off on long solitary walks and I would watch her covertly, too miserable myself to offer more than inarticulate and inadequate comfort.

His letters to us were always full of jokes and gentle reminders to care for our mother – something my brother did a great deal more conscientiously and carefully than I – and he had a delightful old-fashioned way of always ending his letters "From your loving father, Ben." I thought this wonderfully grown up and remember signing my own letters: "From your loving child, Yvonne."

Sometimes I had vivid dreams of before the war and the times he had come home on leave, when we had done exciting things like driving up to London to see a 'Show' with Jessie Matthews and Sonny Hale; or perhaps the Crazy Gang at the Palladium, or Robertson Hare and Tom Walls being silly and losing their trousers. Once, when I was about nine, his ship had to go into for refit and repairs and I was allowed to travel with him from London's East Ham docks to Newcastle, a journey in which I was massively spoilt, and not only by my father. As the ship steamed around the coast through perfect summer weather his cabin steward constantly slipped me cakes from the galleys, encouraged me to play uproarious games in the huge empty playrooms and instructed me in the art of Skittles and Deck Quoits. All this fuelled my determination to go to sea when I grew up and I couldn't understand why my brother wasn't interested in following in father's footsteps. All *he* wanted to do was join the Air Force and be a pilot; something my mother, whose favourite brother had been shot down and killed in nineteen-seventeen, was determined to prevent. However, Fate in the shape of an insignificant little Austrian with a funny moustache intervened, and at seventeen and a half my brother seized his chance to jettison any plans for a career in the navy to go up into the sky; thereby breaking his mother's heart and giving me enormous kudos amongst my female friends. By the time he had his wings I had discovered that while having a handsome brother made a person popular, having a handsome brother who was also a fighter pilot was the icing on the cake.

How my father, a born sailor from a family of seafarers, felt about his son's defection I never knew, although I imagine it must have caused him some hurt or disappointment. I guess it was just his hard luck really, to have a daughter who loved the sea but *couldn't* follow him, and a son who hated it and *wouldn't*. Not that my brother didn't have his reasons; his one and only venture onto the briny had been on the Isle of Wight ferry and he'd managed to be spectacularly sick before it was even out of Portsmouth harbour. He was also sick in cars and on trains and Green Line buses, but never in a 'plane, so it was small wonder that he decided to make a career in the RAF. It must have been something of a bonus for him to have discovered, albeit a trifle late, a way of getting from here to there without throwing up.

* * * * *

By the end of February, although the snow was still with us, it was possible to walk to school, although we arrived there soaking wet, to sit all day in soggy clothes from which arose a gentle steam to mist the classroom windows and Mrs Brown's spectacles. The return home was always accomplished at a smart pace as chilblains began to tingle and burn. The Green Dragon was a welcome sight on those winter evenings, and before I went indoors I always walked around the side of the building, just for the pleasure of looking through a small tear in our parlour curtains. The lamps would be lit, the fire banked up and glowing and the tea things spread on the white-clothed table. On one particular Friday evening I trotted up to the window for my usual peep and was stopped dead in my tracks, my heart hammering wildly and a terrible tide of sickness engulfing me.

My mother – *my mother* – was seated on the couch beneath the window with a man's arms around her!

I was distraught: rooted to the spot temporarily unable to move. Who was he – how *could* she! I began to cry, then finding my legs again I took off in a rush around the building. Bursting through the side door I hurtled pell-mell down the passageway bawling like a Banshee and flung open the parlour door yelling, 'Stop it! Stop it *at once!*'

My near hysterical outburst was met by a bellow of laughter. The next moment I was in my father's arms, his brass buttons digging into my cheek as I soaked his uniform with a torrent of tears, my senses taking in the familiar smell of freshly shaved skin and Bay Rum.

High on excitement and emotion, my memories of that evening are confused. I remember lying curled into a tight ball between my parents and being hugged by both until my brother's return from school, then sitting around the table for a supper of shepherds pie and bread-and-butter pudding, my mother looking young, her eyes sparkling, my father bumping his head on the low beams when he stood and swearing mildly. Then after tea the unpacking of his big leather cabin trunk, always an exciting ceremony with shirts and underclothes and long woollen socks in the top tray and presents buried at the very bottom of the trunk beneath his spare uniform.

My father never brought home the kind of gifts most men might chose for their children; not toys, but lovely strange things: little objects of desire; although I can remember when I was about six becoming the proud possessor of a life-size papier-mâché French bulldog that moved its head menacingly and growled when I pulled the chain attached to its collar. For years I had a lot of fun with that bulldog and any unwary visitor who ventured past the front door. Unfortunately he had eventually to be consigned to the dustbin, his papier-mâché skin crumbling to dust, his ears and feet chewed away by a succession of dogs.

This time there was a most beautiful Chinese Mandarin's robe for me, of a deep midnight blue, the collar and sleeves banded with delicate ivory silk panels and hand embroidered dragons and flowers and Chinese figures; silk to smooth between the fingers and hundreds of pictures to study and marvel at for hours. That there was a rather sinister rust-coloured stain on the back of the lining only served to heighten the mystery and glamour of the gift ... Could it possibly be *blood*? I asked, and my father nodded gravely, answering that was very likely as he'd bought it from the widow of Hoo Flung Dung High, whose husband had disappeared in mysterious circumstances. I believed him and couldn't understand why my brother was so overcome with laughter that he rolled on the floor howling and clutching his ribs.

He had a carved wooden box with an ingenuously hidden spring that took him an age to find. When he'd finally worked out how to open it there were two envelopes inside, each containing a large white five-pound note, so fresh and new that it crackled when unfolded.

For years my brother kept all his most treasured possessions and a secret diary in this box, sure in the knowledge that they were safe from my prying eyes; which just went to show how little he knew, although it did take me all of a dozen frustrating attempts before I'd figured out how it worked.

For once I didn't crow about my cleverness. It was much more satisfying to know that I knew what he didn't want me to know about his daft girlfriends and how often he'd French-kissed Helen Normington in the bus shelter in Bewdley, and that he'd seen Mary O'Rioden's bloomers when she cycled with him to school.

Sadly, I was unable to pry into his adult secrets as he took his box to Burma with him, where it was eaten by termites. It didn't matter anyway as by that time I'd plenty of secrets of my own to keep.

* * * * *

The seven days of my father's leave passed so swiftly that only a few incidents stand out from the rest. One of these was when he took Georgie and me to Kidderminster to see *Pinocchio*; remembered less for the film than the enormous tea we ate at a very posh restaurant afterwards, my father watching us with mingled amusement and disbelief as we demolished a whole plate of hot scones and lardy cake. I had a passion for the Worcestershire lardy cake, which was soft and doughy with a crisp, sugary crust that was most gloriously sticky around the teeth. No lardy I have eaten since has ever achieved that standard of perfection.

To my delight my father showed an immediate liking for Georgie, perhaps recognising in that small boy a kindred spirit, having himself been something of the family Black Sheep. Not only, as his sister-in-law once confided darkly to my mother in my hearing, had he been expelled from King Edward's School in Southampton for some unspecified crime, but had then been despatched by his father a few years later on a one way ticket to Australia.

He addressed Georgie as 'old man' and listened attentively to what he had to say. This was a novelty to Georgie and he blossomed noticeably under this adult interest in himself and his affairs. Now and again I felt a small twinge of jealousy but quickly banished it; time was too precious and I was too happy to waste it on squabbling with Georgie.

But my most vivid memory of that time is the day of the bomb.

Both my parents had gone off early that morning, glad no doubt to have some time together away from us. It was a Saturday and my father was due to return to his ship on the following Monday. Mrs 'Arris was obviously far from thrilled at having me around for the hour or two until I was collected by my aunt and I was warned to keep out of her way and not make a nuisance of myself. My brother of course was above needing such instruction.

When we first heard the drone of the plane he was at the table busy with his homework, whilst I was curled on the couch with my nose buried in the pages of *William and the Outlaws*. Intent on our separate occupations it was a moment or two before we heard the unmistakable sound of a Dornier 217 overhead. We both looked up at the same moment, our faces registering disbelief and excitement in equal measure.

'Bloody Hell!' my brother exploded and leaped for the door with me hard on his heels and together we raced into the yard. There it was, right above us: dark and menacing, flying just below the clouds with that well remembered thumping drone.

Mrs 'Arris laboured from the kitchen to join us; wiping her hands on her apron she demanded, 'Noo then; what you tw'm looking at?'

'That German Bomber,' my brother pointed skyward. 'He

must be lost – he's probably on his way back from Birmingham.'

Had he announced that Attila the Hun and his Hoard were pouring down Furze Hill the effect on Mrs 'Arris could not have been more dramatic; grabbing each of us in a vice-like grip she surged through the pub, shrieking to the Almighty and Mr 'Arris for aid and deliverance.

'Oh! My Gud! Oh my *Gud*! Eli! Eli! Open the cellar! Oh my Gud – save us! We're being barmed! ELI-I-I!'

As Eli heaved open the trap door we were towed down into the cellar, mercifully without sustaining any permanent injury. As we thudded onto the brick floor at the bottom of the steep wooden steps I found myself clasped to Mrs 'Arris' vast bosom and in imminent danger of suffocation. My brother, recoiling in horror from suffering a similar fate, collided with a hanging side of bacon and nearly knocked himself out. Poor Eli sat on the steps sucking his moustache and making soothing clicks of the tongue such as I'd heard him do to his pigs. Gazing with anxious and watery eyes at his palpitating spouse and half-stunned lodger he crooned, 'There noo, doan 'e fuss, Daisy. You'm safe doan 'ere!'

I hauled my purple face from the enveloping bosom to gaze entranced at Mrs 'Arris. Fancy! *Daisy*! Who would have guessed? I caught my brother's eye as he lay on the floor and we both erupted into uncontrollable giggles. Just at that moment there was the unmistakable if distant crump of an exploding bomb, and with one final 'Oh, my Gud!' Mrs 'Arris fell in a heap on the floor, breathing heavily and emitting periodic squeaks rather like those of a homing bat.

Eli knelt beside her patting her hand saying, 'Coom oop, Daisy, coom oop!' and sounding so much like the neighbouring farmer calling up his cows that I had another fit of the giggles.

'Shut up, you!' My brother recovered rapidly and sat up, glaring aggressively at me and using his bossy, "I'm in charge" voice. 'What we need is a paper bag for her to breathe into, like mum did when my engine blew up.'

I stopped giggling and looked around; the only paper bag I could see was caked with dried blood and tied firmly over the head of a very dead hare suspended by its feet from the ceiling; even I balked at getting Mrs 'Arris to breathe into that. 'You could try hitting her,' I suggested helpfully.

'Not likely! Anyway, that's for people having fits or something, you twerp. *She's* just having a funny turn.'

I looked doubtfully at Mrs 'Arris who by now had lapsed into stentorian snores. 'How can you tell the difference?'

He glared again and we lapsed into silence in company with the side of bacon, the dead hare and an even deader and distinctly whiffy pheasant, willing Mrs 'Arris to respond to her husband's entreaties to 'Coom oop, Daisy' and release us from what was becoming an unpleasantly odorous tomb.

But for the timely arrival of my aunt, we would possibly have sat there all day until our parent's return. Under her brisk direction we all joined in heaving Mrs 'Arris to her feet and propelling her up the stairs and into the bar, where my aunt proceeded to pour brandy down her throat until she returned to life with a great splutter and several more 'Oh, my Guds!'

My aunt controlled her mirth until we had left and were well clear of the pub, when she was obliged to sit on a convenient wall and give vent to great shrieks of laughter. 'What a hoot!' she gasped, wiping her eyes. 'How on earth did she get in that state? It wasn't anything either of you did, I hope?'

'Certainly not,' I was offended, 'it was the bomb – she just yelled "Omigud!" and fell on the floor.'

'I wanted to put her head in a paper bag but there wasn't one,' my brother was equally aggrieved.

'Never mind; it was a good idea.' My aunt gave another hoot of laughter. 'It would have been an improvement, wouldn't it?'

We all laughed then, rolling about like barrels in our vulgar mirth over poor Daisy. I loved my aunt at that moment; to have a grown-up descend to one's own level of silliness was very satisfying.

When my parents returned that evening she insisted that we recount the whole episode again from beginning to end, with the result that for the remaining two days of his leave my father was unable to look Mrs 'Arris in the eye. Later that night when I was in bed I could hear his spasmodic explosions of mirth mingled with my mother's laughter. I thought that perhaps it had all been worth while being just a little bit frightened by the sight of the bomber and the sound of that explosion if it had made so many people laugh. The next morning I asked my brother if he'd been frightened too and he looked at me with scorn.

'Of course not, dopey. In a couple of years I'll be up there and getting my own back.'

And of course, as it happened he did just that.

* * * * *

On Sunday evening my father asked us if we would like to help him pack. Rather subdued and glum at this reminder that his leave was almost over we took a drawer apiece from the chest and began to sort his belongings into piles on the bed. When we had filled the top tray of his case with shirts and thick roll-neck jerseys, the long white socks and warm underwear, my brother shoved me towards the wardrobe. 'You get his spare uniform out and lay it on the bed and I'll fold it.'

I opened the wardrobe door and gazed for a moment at my mother's dresses and winter coat. 'It isn't here.'

'Of course it is, stupid! Look properly.'

'I have, pig face – look for yourself!'

'Dumb broad,' he was fond of American gangster films and fancied himself as James Cagney, 'just do as I say or I'll fill you full of lead!' He came to stand beside me, and moving my mother's clothes aside peered into the wardrobe. 'They have to be here *somewhere*.' He looked at me suspiciously, 'are you playing one of your daft tricks?'

I kicked his shin hard and took off down the stairs calling sweetly, 'Daddy, we can't find your spare uniform!'

My father followed me back up the stairs and looked suspiciously at the sight of his son apparently dancing a hornpipe. 'Now then, what are you up to? This is no time to be playing silly beggars. Come on: where have you put it?'

My brother rubbed his shin and shot me a look of pure malevolence. 'It's her – she's always up to something.'

My father crooked a beckoning finger at me. 'Come here. Where have you hidden it?'

Prudently I kept my distance. 'I wouldn't even *think* of doing such a thing,' I said primly. 'Only a *really* stupid person like that idiot boy would believe I might!'

I think that my brother might have killed me at that moment, but for the arrival of my mother on the scene. She looked thoughtfully at me as my father explained, and secure for once in my innocence I gazed soulfully back. 'It's not me. Really it isn't.'

She sighed and gave a resigned shrug. 'He wouldn't; she would but she hasn't! So where is it?'

We all shrugged.

After a fruitless search of every likely and unlikely nook and cranny my father was a very worried man. The idea he might have to return to his ship minus his spare uniform and explain that he had lost it in a pub was beginning to assume alarming proportions.

But he was not the only victim of the phantom pilferer. During the search my mother discovered that her watch and a ring were also missing. Setting her lips in a way that we knew only too well presaged trouble with a capital T, she sallied forth to inform mine hosts that we had been burgled and would they please telephone for the police.

There followed a long period of muffled conversation, interspersed by several loud "Oh, my Guds" from Mrs 'Arris before my mother reappeared bearing my father's uniform, her watch and ring, managing to look amused and embarrassed at one and the same time.

We leaped upon her demanding: 'Where *were* they? Did Mr 'Arris catch the burglar?'

'Never you mind; they are back and that is all that matters,' was the unsatisfactory reply, then she gave my father one of Those Looks and they went upstairs deep in low voiced conversation.

Straining our ears we caught the odd word: 'Poor woman … he said it must have been the gold braid … like a Jackdaw …

not at all well … kleptomaniac….'

We rushed for the Chambers Dictionary, but as we'd never heard the word before and it never occurred to us it began with Klept and not Clap we were doomed to remain in ignorance, until my mother finally gave in to our pestering some days later. Charitably she explained away Mrs 'Arris's little problem as being caused by the shock she suffered the day of the bomb, and forbade us to mention it again. We had our suspicions that she was fibbing a bit but reluctantly promised to say nothing. However that didn't stop my brother amusing himself for some time afterwards by going about the place with an imaginary magnifying glass investigating what he named in Sherlockian terms as The Case of the Naked Sailor.

* * * * *

Buried somewhere in the very deepest recesses of my memory are those last moments when my father's train pulled slowly out of the station at Shrub Hill; moments almost too painful to be taken out and spoken of even after more than sixty years. The tears in my father's eyes as I stumbled alongside the moving train in a state of terror calling, 'Don't go, Daddy. Don't go!' My mother catching me at the end of the platform and holding me clasped in her arms as we watched his carriage out of sight.

Of the return home I remember nothing but a sense of desolation and an aching void, like a hunger deep inside my chest. We never spoke about that day. I think my mother was wise enough to know that some things cannot be turned over and examined and made safe; that some pain has to be lived with; that this pain was a necessary and unavoidable part of loving.

THE VILLAGE STORE

Rats...

'That there bomb them Germans dropped on Stourport made a nasty mess.' As usual Miss Alice knew every detail of any happening within a twenty-mile radius of the village. 'No dead, though.' She sounded regretful.

It was blessed half-term and we were all four perched on stools before the counter, nibbling on fragments of broken biscuit, listening while Miss Alice dispensed all the gossip about everyone in and around the village. It was the quiet time between the early morning rush for bread and gravy browning and the late morning pop in for "Five Woodbines, please" and a nice chat. In the Forest there was a strict segregation between serious and social shopping. We knew when we would be welcome and when to stay out of sight.

'Do'an' you tell nobody this...' Miss Alice hitched herself over the counter and lowered her voice. We all perked up, as this was the usual prelude to an extra spicy bit of news. 'I found rat dirt's in me flour!'

We were disappointed. Rats, with or without their dirts, were hardly news around this part of the world. On one memorable occasion my father had found himself sharing the privy with one. There was no contest about who had the right of occupancy when the rat was summarily ejected out of the door by the swift application of a large naval boot to its rear.

'Just pick 'em out,' suggested Georgie after some thought, 'no one'll know.'

'It's them there 'ealth inspectors – nosy boogers; they'm allus comin' around on the sly.' Miss Alice gave a loud disparaging sniff. 'It be this bloomin' war – never 'ad to bother wi' the likes o' they before.'

Again Georgie mulled over her problem in silence for a few minutes. 'I could bring me ferret,' he offered at last, ''e'd soon sort 'em, good n' proper.'

Miss Alice looked alarmed. 'I don't want no blood over my store shed; more trouble than the rat dirt's that 'ud be!'

'Oh there wouldn't be much blood!' Georgie was airily confident. 'See, I let me ferret go inside an' leaves the door open so 'e c'n chase 'em out; then as they runs inter the yard we 'its 'em on the 'ead.'

Mavis squealed loudly. '*I'm* not hitting *anything* on the head!'

'Twerp!' Georgie snorted derisively, 'you'm scared of yer own shadow!' He hesitated a moment then added nonchalantly. 'I could always bring Snap.'

Even I blanched at this. Snap belonged to Little Senior and was a small mongrel of such uncertain temperament that even strong men gave him a wide berth. Pass too close to the Little's fence when Snap was off his chain and he'd have you through the palings. However, he certainly was a marvellous ratter.

Miss Alice shared my misgivings. 'You bring that devil you keep 'im on a lead! Doan you let 'im near me.'

''Cause not – I'll keep 'im on a long rope; you won't 'ave no rat dirt's after me ferret an' Snap's bin around.'

'Probably none of us'll have any ankles either!' I grumbled, far from happy about this venture. I'd never been afraid of any dog in my whole life before, but Snap was definitely something much more sinister and lethal than your common-or-garden canine. 'Anyway, your dad most likely won't let you bring him.'

''Cause 'e will; 'e knows Snap's all right wi' me.'

After further considerable discussion of ways and means and reassurances to Miss Alice, who was more than doubtful about Georgie's plan, arrangements were made for the following day and we departed to our various homes to beg sandwiches and a bottle of milk or water. Although the weather was only marginally above freezing we wanted to make the most of a bright and reasonably dry day to be out of doors; experience having told us that if you hung around the house too long during a school holiday, *someone* always managed to find something for you to do.

Pleasantly exhausted and satisfied after our afternoon of tree climbing and impromptu races in the fresh air, we returned reluctantly home in time for tea. Mrs Little invited me to sit down at their table and I jumped at the chance. I liked Georgie's mum a lot. She was a tiny woman who kept her brood in reasonable order with the aid, when necessary, of a large wooden spoon. Despite her unerring aim with this they all had an enormous affection for and pride in "our mam." She treated me no differently from her own offspring and would on occasions absentmindedly fetch me one with the spoon, which always brought a concerted shout of 'Yer got the wrong one agin, mam!'

I didn't mind; I enjoyed being an honorary Little, even if it was occasionally rather painful, and I liked Pa Little, who sat in his big wooden armchair in the crowded kitchen, letting the tide of humanity flow around him and from time to time plucking the odd passing child onto his knee. He didn't say much; just the occasional "Oo, arr" and he smoked a foul-smelling pipe stuffed with thick black tobacco. My mother said she always knew when I had been in their cottage because my hair smelled of smoke. Fortunately she couldn't tell the difference between Mr Little's black shag and Mrs 'Arris's Woodbines.

* * * * *

The following morning we met as arranged at the den. Georgie had Snap well under control with a length of hemp that could have done duty as a shoreline for the Titanic and Nelson his ferret was up his jumper. We made Georgie walk well in front of us so that we could keep a weather eye on the ubiquitous Snap, who kept looking back at us and curling his lip. He really was a horrible dog.

On our arrival at the shop Miss Alice gave Snap a wide berth and took us into the back yard to her store shed. 'I'll be in the shop if you need me,' she said unlocking the door, then added, 'Mind – no blood on the vit'uls!'

At this Mavis's courage deserted her, and she disappeared into the adjacent privy to watch the proceedings through the holes in the door.

Georgie handed me Nelson instructing: 'You git in and put 'im on the floor be the sacks, then you'm better get up on them boxes quick, 'cos them rats is goin' ter run like 'ell when 'e gits goin'!'

Retrieving the acrobatic Nelson from my left sleeve I did as ordered. From my viewpoint high up in the boxes of tinned veg I felt a bit as I imagined the Romans might have whilst waiting for the Christians to be thrown to the lions. For several seconds nothing happened, then suddenly all hell was let loose as Nelson did his stuff.

Snap was aptly named; as the rats fled through the open door into the confines of the small yard he was on them; snap-toss, snap-toss. Dead bodies flew in all directions. Georgie wielded a bloody stick and yelled encouragement and Mavis screamed from her vantage point in the privy, whilst Mickey, in order to dodge the flying rats, positively levitated over the fence, landing in a bed of nettles and adding his howls of agony to the general cacophony.

It was all over in less than a minute, the rats ceased to run through the door and Nelson's sleek form oozed from the shed. Looking justifiably smug he sniffed delicately at the triumphant Snap where he sat with lolling, blood-soaked tongue, surrounded by an untidy ring of corpses. I jumped down from my perch and we all cheered like mad, even Mickey.

At that moment, attracted no doubt by all the noise, there appeared through the back gate the corpulent form of P.C. Archibald Bunn, known to us of course as A Bum.

'Noo then, noo then – what's gooing on 'ere?'

Georgie jumped and let go of the towrope, allowing Snap to shoot joyously across the yard and fasten his teeth on A Bum's toe cap.

Georgie was on a high. Hopping from one foot to the other he crowed, 'We'm just got all them rats what's bin shittin' in the flour!'

A Bum cuffed him smartly across the back of the head, making Georgie's teeth rattle and his eyes roll. 'Noo then – manners! Noo bad language!' He looked down and appeared for the first time to notice the growling appendage to his boot, 'and get that little booger off my bloody foot afore I takes me 'and to yer arse!'

It took the combined efforts of Georgie and me to lever Snap's jaws from A Bum's footwear and drag him snarling ferociously to the far end of the yard. With a last thump on Georgie's ear and the order to 'get that there mad booger back 'ome' the denizen of the law took his stately and unhurried departure, and we all took a concerted deep breath of relief.

'The trouble with people,' Georgie rubbed his ear and stared morosely after A Bum's wide uniformed rear, 'is they tells yer not ter do somethin', then do's it themselves!'

We shovelled up the corpses with the coal scoop and threw them on the compost heap, before retrieving Mavis from the privy and Mickey from the nettles. With Snap safely shut up in Mavis's late place of safety and Nelson again stuffed into Georgie's jersey, we passed our hands under the yard tap and trooped into the shop to be congratulated by Miss Alice.

She did us proud. There was a cone of goodies each – an inch or so of lemonade powder at the bottom, then humbugs, violet cachous, peppermints and on top a chocolate toffee. Nelson had a biscuit and Snap a bone in a paper bag for when he got home.

Later, in the den with our feet up to the fire, dipping bright yellow fingers into the end of our paper cones to retrieve the last grains of lemonade powder, we agreed that despite Georgie's clouts and Mickey's nettle bumps, it had been an altogether most satisfying day.

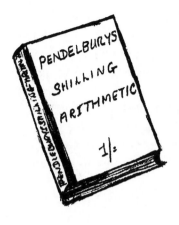

... and Moles

All good things must come to an end and nothing lasts forever. On our return to school after the half-term we were shocked to learn that Georgie, myself, and three other unfortunates had been moved into Mr Mole's class, some lucky fourteen year olds having escaped during the holiday. As Mr Mole didn't like spaces on his benches they had to be filled and we were next in line. To say we were horrified would be a massive understatement. Normally only the final year was passed in the top form and we had felt safe until after the summer holidays.

'Bloody 'ell fire!' Georgie picked gloomily at a scab on his knee as we took our places at morning prayers. 'I ain't got me strength up yet fer that ol' looney!'

As luck would have it Mr Mole was at his most volatile on this particular morning; a week's absence from beating the Word of the Lord into his hapless charges had him in near frenetic mood. Prayer books and blackboard dusters flew, and we were all roundly cursed and threatened, if not with hell-fire at least with Mole-fire. When the lucky ones had escaped to their classrooms, leaving some thirty hapless pupils to his tender mercies, he crooked a bony finger at the huddle of his new victims now cowering in the back row. 'Doon the front, where I can see you!' he intoned in a voice of indescribable menace.

Carefully avoiding eye contact with Mole we shuffled into the places willingly vacated by five of our fellows. He prowled up and down before us for a moment before suddenly poking a lanky lad in the chest. 'Noo then, 'Artley; give us a poem!'

Poor Tom Hartley gaped like a stranded fish and looked wildly around. Beside me I felt Georgie shift nervously. 'A–a *poem*?' Tom's voice was a shrill squeak.

'Yes, A POEM!' Mole rolled his eyes to heaven. 'Get on with it!'

Tom swallowed hard:

'Ickerydickererydockthemowsrunuptheclo –'

'Rotten!' Mole cuffed him vigorously and turned his attention to the next in line. 'Noo then, Emily Drippin': lets 'ear *you*!'

Now Emily Dripping was something else again. Big, she was; a beefy-faced wench with small mean eyes who could throw a hefty punch when annoyed. She it was who had imparted to me her own unexpurgated version of the facts of life, which at the time I had found incomprehensible and frankly ludicrous; as if grown-up people would voluntarily do anything so bizarre. She'd belted me when I called her a lying cow, so now I watched with some pleasure as she flinched, shut her piggy orbs and managed a whole line of "Wake me early, mother darling, for I'm to be Queen of the May," before Mole's tortured yell of ''Orrible! 'Orrible! Shut up!' halted the flow and the redoubtable Emily burst into tears.

Satisfied, Mole passed to Georgie, who shuffled his feet and shook his head hopelessly.

'Don't known none, sir.'

'Seven years in this school and you "Don't know none?"' Georgie got cuffed twice; then it was my turn.

'Ha! The H'admiral's daughter!' I narrowed my eyes: bloody cheek. Who did he think he was? 'What are we goin' to hear from *you* – the Death of Nelson?' He chortled loudly at his own joke.

Now I was a normally inattentive and lazy pupil, always to be found somewhere around the bottom of the class, but I did have one talent: a phenomenal memory for verse. At Miss Lee's Academy, where the learning by heart of long narrative poems and large chunks of Shakespeare were an important part of the curriculum, this had been a major asset. Now I took a deep breath, looked Mole straight in the eye and gave him the whole of Polonius's advice to his son, complete with appropriate gestures.

I finished and there fell one of those silences during which one could have heard the proverbial pin drop. I waited for the yell of fury, knowing I'd been what my mother would call too clever by half. But he'd asked for poetry and poetry he'd got – the very best to be found, according to Neuter.

Mr Mole bent his bony frame until his eyes were on a level with mine. 'Is that what *you* calls poetry?' he asked, menacingly, almost licking his lips in anticipation of making another female dissolve into tears. Secure in my knowledge that I was right I answered loudly, 'Shakespeare thought it was.'

Mole let out a loud hissing breath and someone behind me

breathed a terrified 'Oh, *Gawd*!' My bravado left me and like a rabbit caught in headlights I stared, suddenly trapped and witless, into the inky depths of his narrowed eyes.

Suddenly he shot up to his full height and glared around the class. 'Noo then! I'll bet none of *you* ignorant boogers knew that, did you?'

There was the sound of some thirty pent-up breaths being expired and a chorus of, 'No, sir!'

'Right, so now you knows: when I asks for poetry, *proper* poetry is what I wants and gets!'

Delighted with having demonstrated his somewhat tardy familiarity with the Bard, he ordered us to get on with page ten of Pendlebury's Shilling Arithmetic before stalking off to his desk to read the *Daily Mirror*, completely forgetting to terrorise Alfie Evans, the last one in our line-up, who showed his gratitude by giving me a piece of his bacon sandwich at dinnertime.

* * * * *

Mr Mole proved to have a simple method of teaching: one that afforded him the greatest leisure and minimum of input, while presenting his pupils with the greatest difficulty in learning anything at all. It went something like this:

The teaching of Arithmetic meant the whole class worked *en masse* through the aforementioned Pendlebury's Shilling Arithmetic, page by page, irrespective of individual ability or whether all or any understood what it was all about. Under this system there were many who passed the entire year in his class to emerge at the end of their captivity as fourteen year old wage-earning adults no more advanced in the intricacies of Mathematics as presented in Pendlebury's shilling Arithmetic than the day they'd arrived.

Writing consisted of penning pages of pothooks on ruled paper with scratching nibs dipped in gritty ink, a recipe for disaster if ever there was one; the resultant mess generally ripped to shreds by Mole at the end of the day and followed by much brisk smacking of heads. Reading and Scripture doubled up and proved the occasion for pieces of chalk, blackboard rubbers and ferocious curses being flung more or less accurately at anyone rash enough to hesitate too long over a word. History consisted of the reciting of dates and the ascension of kings, becoming progressively incident free as after a few weeks even the dullest knew the lot by heart, from King Canute to King George the Sixth.

Geography was the tricky one and the stuff of which nightmares were made.

On the far wall, much too close for comfort to Mole's desk, hung a large map of the world. Standing on the dais with a bamboo cane in his hand he would yell a victim's name, together with a city, sea, island etc., and the chosen one would then scurry out and attempt to locate it on the map before Mole's patience ran out and the cane descended with a thwack.

Each day was as crazy as anything Lewis Carroll might have thought up, and at going-home time we left the school feeling mentally and physically battered. The village children viewed it as nerve-wracking but normal; to most of the evacuees it was a preview of hell.

That any of the local children emerged at the end of their year in Mole's class still sane and able to read and write has to be viewed as a minor miracle. That this particular group of evacuees returned home at the end of the war without precipitating an East Anglian boom in homicidal maniacs or gibbering idiots can only be attributed to the wartime child's stoicism in the face of adversity.

As we walked home after our first day of Trial by Mole, Georgie and me recounted with some bravado the day's events to a horrified Mickey and Mavis.

'I just shan't go into his class.' Mavis was emphatic. 'I shall tell mummy and she'll keep me at home.'

'Me too,' echoed her brother, his lower lip trembling. Georgie patted his shoulder reassuringly.

''S'all right. You'm ain't got ter go fer another two or three years – the war'll be over be then an' you'm 'ull be back 'ome agin.'

I grumbled, 'That can't be soon enough for me, I'd go tonight if I could!' – then realised that although the end of the war would release me from Mole's clutches, it would mean leaving the Forest and all the freedom and friends it offered. I tried to imagine life without Georgie, without the den, without dozy Mavis and naïve Mickey, without Miss Alice and her gossip and broken biscuits.

An awful tide of sadness rolled over me. Half of me wanted the war to end, to get away from Mole and for my dad to come home, but the other half wanted it to go on forever. I felt confused and unhappy and picked a quarrel so that I could run ahead of them all and find a tree to sit in and brood alone over my rotten day.

Perched high above the pathway in the wet and slimy branches of an oak, I watched my friends pass, hating them because they were laughing and didn't seem to miss me at all. I sat on snivelling loudly while the damp oozed through my knickers and my bottom ached with cold. I would, I vowed, cut my hair and run away to sea rather than spend another day in

Mole's classroom. Eventually, shivering and with chattering teeth, I inched down onto the path and limped home on feet stiff with cold and swollen with chilblains.

My mother looked hard at my no doubt sullen expression as I dumped my sandwich box on the kitchen table. She asked, 'Did you enjoy your day?'

'No.'

'Never mind, have a hot cake.'

I wouldn't be comforted and glowered at the offered cake. 'I had a row with Georgie and I hate stupid Mavis and dopey Mickey – and Hitler!'

She said 'Have two cakes!' then added with an infuriatingly knowing smile, 'It's all right; you're just growing up.'

Juggling the two hot cakes in my hands I stamped away into the outhouse and sat on a soggy hay bale to complain about the unfairness of life to a couple of disinterested cats. I hated old Dan Mole and I'd rather die than sit in his class every day, I told them, and I didn't want to grow up either. Being almost thirteen wasn't much fun; being properly grown up would be no fun at all.

The cats just stared back and I wept and raged and cried for my father to come home and hug me and make me laugh and tell me that tomorrow would be a better day.

THE GIBBET.

Dead and Buried

Somehow I struggled through that winter, miserably resigned to the ranting of the Mad Mole, chilblains, boils, nits and impetigo. Nitty Nora the school nurse scraped regularly and diligently through our heads, then shook her own over our scabby chins and eyebrows. We all went about with hair odoriferous from weekly applications of Derbac soap, our faces daubed with gentian violet, giving us the appearance of diminutive ancient Britons who'd overdone the woad.

A cold sunless Easter came and went and with it my thirteenth birthday. I still had mixed feelings about that; I had no strong desire to work hard and pass exams, viewing with distaste the approaching time when I would be required to go out into the world and earn a living; even less attractive was the long-term possibility of getting married. Emily Dripping's dire revelations on the married state had definitely put me off that for the foreseeable future, if not for life, added to which I most

certainly did not want an adult version of my brother around the
place, bossing me about and wanting his dinner on the table.

Georgie and I talked over these problems from time to time;
he shared my apprehension at the idea of marriage, stating
firmly that he wasn't going to have some ol' girl pinchin' *his*
wages each week and having babies all over the place.

The subject was raised again one mild spring evening when
we were all in the den cooking a second tea of sausages and
fried bread, and Mickey offered confidently, 'I'm going to be a
sailor, so I shan't need to get married. I'll just have a girl in
every port!'

Georgie grinned. ''Es comin' on, in't 'e?' he said admir-
ingly.

'Don't encourage him.' I was offended and gave Georgie a
shove. 'He's practically calling my father a lecher!'

This word was always popping up in the books my aunt
borrowed from the library in W.H. Smith's, so I'd looked it up
in her Concise Oxford English Dictionary, which being both
Oxford and Concise had to be right. *A lewd and lustful man* it
said. So that was that. 'Some sailors,' I said loftily, 'behave
like gentlemen.'

Mavis gazed dreamily into space. 'I want to get married and
have lots and lots of dear little babies.'

Georgie and I made sick noises and nearly fell off our stool
laughing. 'You'm joost coom an' live in our 'ouse fer a bit and
you'm soom fergit *that* one!' he spluttered and I dug him in the
ribs.

'Remember that time your Jenny did it in your pa's pocket?'

The memory sent us off into such shrieks of mirth that even

Mavis had to join with us; we howled until it became too painful to bear and only the smell of burning sausages brought us to our senses. When we'd scraped off the worst of the black bits and sat chewing on the remains, I rather unkindly told Mavis what she'd have to do in order to get all those babies. She went pale and heaved on her mouthful of charred meat. Georgie looked sympathetic and said encouragingly, 'You'm cud always adopt a few.'

This seemed to cheer her up no end although I couldn't see the point of going to all that trouble. Babies did disgusting things and smelt pretty terrible, wherever you got them from.

* * * * *

Slowly spring gave way to summer and with the long warm evenings we began to range further a-field in search of bird's eggs and butterflies and the fragrant early pink and white mushrooms our mother loved to have with her morning bacon. It was on one of these expeditions that we strayed onto the estate of some local bigwig and came face to face with the gamekeeper's gibbet.

We had been following a broad rutted track through the forest for several hundred yards before rounding a bend and halting before a heavy five-bar gate. Nailed to a tree beside this was a white board with black painted letters warning:

PRIVATE
TRESPASSERS WILL BE PROSCECUTED

Beneath this dire pronouncement, crow, weasel, rat and magpie hung from the wooden fence rails, strung by their necks and with little paws and claws dangling.

Shocked to the core of our suburbanite little souls, the Harpers and I gazed in horror at the rows of little corpses as they swayed gently in the breeze, making a dry rustling sound like stealthy footsteps.

Mavis hid her face in her hands, 'Oh, how horrid!'

Georgie looked baffled. 'S'only them li'l vermin boogers; keeper 'angs 'em up ter warn the others.'

Logic wasn't my strong point but even I knew no wild animals or birds were going to use a gate to gain entry to someone's land, let alone read any warning notices. I said, 'That's stupid; animals don't *think* like that. Some rotten keeper just does it to show how clever he is.'

Georgie gave a derisive snort. 'Don't make no difference, do it? They'm still dead!'

I digested this in silence. He was right of course, but there was something so ghoulish and disgusting about those pathetic little cadavers that I couldn't bear the thought of just passing by and leaving them to continue rotting away. There surfaced in my mind the remembrance of the death and subsequent ceremonial burial some years before of my brother's pet goldfish. I'd been sad about the poor dead fish but the funeral had been most enjoyable.

My father had wanted to cremate it in the kitchen boiler but my brother insisted on a proper internment, so we'd put it in a tissue paper lined cardboard box; my father had dug a deep hole by the summerhouse and we'd buried it, chanting prayers and scattering flowers over the grave. The whole thing had been the most tremendous fun. 'How about,' I suggested tentatively, 'if we cut them down and buried them?'

All three stared at me blankly. Impatiently I mimed digging a hole. 'You know – with a proper funeral and all that.'

A wide grin split Georgie's freckled face. 'Make ol' keeper

bloody mad, that would!'

Mavis, her eyes shinning asked, 'Could we sing hymns and that?'

'Of course – and put flowers on the graves.' I knew that would get her. 'Come on then...' With a flourish I produced from my knickers pocket the penknife I'd won from my brother in a game of Pontoon. 'We can make a graveyard behind the den; we can have services and make crosses and things.'

We rolled up our jerseys to making carrying pouches then, cutting down all the corpses, distributed them between us. Filled with enthusiasm for our new crusade we made for home.

As we reached Keepers Cottage we could hear Mrs Harper playing the piano in the parlour. While she was occupied and out of sight of the back garden we left Mavis as lookout while the rest of us crept around the back of the house and helped ourselves to forks and trowels from the potting shed.

Working together we excavated a whole row of individual graves and were about to start the actual burials when Mavis held everything up by insisting that the corpses must have shrouds. For a time we were baffled and the whole thing ground to a halt until she had the bright idea of using cake doilies, volunteering to pilfer them from the dining room sideboard. Georgie said them boogering rats would look silly with frills around their necks but I though the doilies were a good idea, and for once sided with Mavis.

It took a lot of concentration to fit the shrouds, as some of the cadavers were pretty old and bits kept breaking off, but eventually they were all laid to rest and by teatime there was a neat row of graves behind the pigsty, each marked by a wooden cross and bearing the legend R.I.P in black crayon.

Fired with enthusiasm we began to wage war upon the keeper.

He was a young chap, dedicated to his work on the estate and was no doubt infuriated by our forays into his territory. As fast as he hung up new victims, no matter how often he changed the location to different trees and fences we would find them, cut them down and, stuffing our haul of decomposing bodies into our jerseys, race for home to give them decent burial.

As Mavis observed sentimentally, they looked really sweet with their little heads peeking from the top of Mrs Harper's doilies, their paws or claws poked through the lace. Funerals were conducted with taste and dignity, apart from the usual initial unseemly altercation about who was to be the officiating priest and who the mere acolytes. As a member, albeit reluctant, of the church choir, Georgie had sneaked a surplice which he seldom relinquished without a struggle. He liked processing around the graveyard, crossing himself copiously and intoning 'Ashes to ashes; doost to doost, if the Lord won't take 'im, the devil moost', while the rest of us tagged behind swinging censers made from cracked flower pots full of dry smouldering grass in lieu of incense.

As time went by, collecting the corpses became increasingly hazardous and sometimes downright painful, with long periods spent crouched in the undergrowth to ensure that the coast was clear, and a whack from the keeper's stick if we made a mistake and it wasn't.

He was pretty fly, that keeper. One evening a few weeks after our first foray into his territory we were dismayed to find his murder victims firmly attached to the fence with pieces of stout wire. We stood looking at each other, totally nonplussed by this unexpected turn of events. 'We'm never goin' ter git them off there,' Georgie observed eventually and we all gave a concerted sigh.

'Er, we could, you know – pull their bodies hard and then...' Mickey's voice died away as we all turned and glared at him.

'This isn't the bloody French Revolution!' I was furious. 'We can't bury them properly without their heads!'

Georgie was thoughtful. 'I s'pose we could put the 'eads on agin after – joost poke 'em down a bit more into the paper.'

Mavis stamped her foot. 'Shut up, you horrible boy! What we need is some wire cutters.'

It was so unusual to hear Mavis say anything intelligent, let alone useful, that for a moment we were all rendered speechless.

'Where from?' asked Mickey eventually.

We all looked at Georgie.

'Oh, no!' he shook his head. 'Don' you look at me – my dad'd kill me!'

'We shall have to *buy* some.' My mind was working rapidly. 'I'll get my brother to find out how much they cost, then we'll have to save some of our pocket money each week until we've enough.'

Mavis volunteered: 'I get ninepence and Mickey gets sixpence.'

Georgie brightened and deadheaded my arm. 'I gets a shillin' fer the choir on Sunday an' another threepence when there's a weddin' or a funeral. What about you?'

'A shilling – that's if I haven't broken or lost anything'

He said cautiously, 'We'll 'ave to keep a *bit* back fer sweets.'

'We can't spend more than half on sweets 'cause of the ration so we can put the rest in a tin until we've enough.' Mavis was getting bossy. She put her hands on her hips and gave us the evil eye, 'all right?'

We agreed.

* * * * *

The wire cutters were four and ninepence. We backslid a bit on the sweets, penny whistles, tops and other tempting items in Miss Alice's store, so although Georgie sung his heart out at two weddings and Tom Hartley's grandfather's funeral it was almost four weeks before my brother, first sworn to secrecy, was handed the precious collection of coppers to purchase the cutters.

When we finally recommenced our mission of mercy we had a rich haul. From a half dozen different gallows scattered about the estate woods we collected twenty-seven corpses in one afternoon, most of which were admittedly pretty decomposed and some downright whiffy. We extended the graveyard around the side of the den. Mavis stole a whole packet of new doilies from the sideboard and in order to speed up the manufacture of crosses, Mickey "borrowed" a paring knife from the rack of Mrs Harper's gleaming, stainless-steel kitchen implements.

How we managed to carry on such a large-scale operation without attracting attention from the adults was something of a mystery. Georgie's ma was probably just glad to see the back of him and although mine did occasionally comment on the odd odour given off when my jerseys hit the wash tub, "out of sight, out of mind" must have been the motto for all three mothers.

Left in peace we tended our dead. Apart from the graveyard being desecrated once by a large incontinent dog, nothing interfered with our rescue mission and we continued our raids while the keeper continued to do his best to thwart us. Poor chap, we must have aggravated him beyond all endurance until finally, after many weeks of torment, he Took Steps.

* * * * *

On a hot July morning just before the end of term, when all we wanted was to be about our unlawful business in fields and forest but were instead crowded into our benches waiting for the Mad Mole to appear, we four at last met our Waterloo.

Sweeping in and uttering his usual yell of 'QUIET!' Mr Mole, instead of launching straight into the Lord's Prayer, stood for a full minute in absolute silence, surveying his charges with a jaundiced eye. Nobody moved a muscle.

Something Was Up.

Still in silence, cane clasped behind his back he began to walk up and along each row then, having completed his tour and reduced everyone to a quivering jelly, returned to his desk to indulge in another period of glaring from beneath twitching brows.

'Some of you,' his voice when it finally came was a menacing whisper. ''ave been h'interfering with the duties of Mister Tennant's Gamekeeper!'

My heart crashed somewhere around my kneecaps.

'IT WILL STOP AS FROM THIS MOMENT!'

The cane descended with a whack on the desk. Fortunately *everyone* leaped about six inches in the air so that we were just part of the general terror and even Mavis's scream went unnoticed.

'...because,' he continued, 'if anyone so mooch as sets foot in them woods agin' I will personally string them up by their skin on the SCHOOL RAILINGS!'

* * * * *

It was a gloomy foursome who gathered that evening in the den. 'What we goin' ter do now?' asked Georgie, of no one in particular. 'I ain't riskin' that ol' Mole gettin 'is 'ands on *me*.'

We all murmured our assent.

'Rotten keeper; anybody would think he was catching the ruddy things to eat them.' I wound up the gramophone and put on *Ain't it Grand to be Blooming Well Dead*, which seemed appropriate for the occasion. 'Now we can't have anymore funerals.'

'We could go looking for squashed ones,' suggested Mavis. 'Or get mice off the cats.'

We all shook our heads. 'Wouldn't be the same,' said Mickey.

And of course it never was the same. We tended the graves and put fresh flowers on the little mounds, but our hearts were no longer in the task and by the time the summer holidays began we were already exploring fresh fields and pastures new.

My brother bought the wire cutters from us; parting with half-a-crown after a great deal of haggling. This we spent on lines, hooks and weights for putting down eel nightlines in the river.

It was a grisly and dangerous business despatching our catches the following day with the paring knife, and once Georgie got his thumb bitten; but very tasty the eels were when skinned and fried and squashed between large hunks of fresh baked bread.

Odds ...

Changes were in the air.

My mother and brother had made two or three trips to London during July and August, leaving me with my aunt and young cousins. I enjoyed staying with my aunt and even got to quite like the baby, which says a lot for his charm. His brother at seven and a bit followed me everywhere, hanging upon my every word and trotting a few paces behind the four of us wherever we went, watching all we did with flattering attention until eventually we graciously allowed him into the den. I think we all looked on him as a kind of mascot, although I went off him for a short while after he was sick all over me one night in our shared bed. But as Georgie pointed out, being sick was the sort of thing that couldn't be helped and might happen to anyone.

My aunt was a happy-go-lucky, very relaxed person and never minded how many children were in the house. When she went shopping in Kidderminster or Bewdley or Stourport she was often accompanied by her own children and our gang of four trailing behind her like so many Raggle Taggle Gypsies O.

We would stagger back at the end of these expeditions laden

with shopping for half the village. At each drop-off point there would be a pause for the obligatory cup of tea and piece of cake or biscuit, so that our final arrival back home saw a concerted rush for the privy, each child desperate to get there first to relieve a bursting bladder.

All but Georgie: when he felt the need he just peed in the hedge.

* * * * *

Something about my aunt that I found endlessly fascinating was her completely unselfconscious and natural habit of flirting with every man she met. She did it with the postman, the bus conductor, my father, Georgie's father and even my brother. I asked my mother about it once and she said airily that she thought Emily was just born that way; letting go the fascinating snippet that my aunt had at the age of sixteen flirted her way into the army in 1915 and within six months was in France keeping up the morale of any number of handsome young Subalterns at a base camp in Amiens.

This all sounded terribly romantic and I studied her carefully, mentally filing away bits I thought might come in useful at a later date. In an unguarded moment I confided my ambition to my brother.

'Some hope you've got!' was his crushing reply. 'She has IT – *you've* got about as much IT as a squashed banana!'

I didn't even bother to answer him. Somehow I just knew in my bones that one day he would have to eat his words. I may not have had IT at thirteen, but by the time I turned sixteen I was doing pretty well – and moreover doing it with most of his friends.

* * * * *

Whatever midsummer madness came over the Vicar that made him conscript Georgie and me into taking charge of the toy and bookstall at the village fête must remain forever a mystery. At first reluctant to do anything that smacked of hard work but too cowardly to refuse point-blank, we quickly realised the possible advantage to be gained from getting first crack at the goods before the general public descended upon them. A very nice set of slim leather-bound Kipling's, two Radio Fun Annuals and an almost complete conjuring set came my way. Georgie scorned the books but did well in the peashooter, catapult and Roy Rogers' rifle department. We also raised a lot of money for the Spitfire Fund by the simple expedient of putting a half-Nelson on any child rash enough to pause before our array of goods, then keeping up the pressure until he or she parted with hard cash for a book or toy.

Adults were wooed with winsome smiles or challenging stares, depending on their reaction to our 'Buy something to help build a Spitfire' sales pitch. Even my mother parted with good money for an ancient cookery book with split covers. I thought this jolly sporting of her as she cooked by instinct and used neither cookery book nor scales. To this day I do the same, which could account for my own daughter's frustration years later when she would ask: 'How much flour?' and I'd reply, 'Oh, about a handful, I should think.'

This could be the reason her large and healthy family frequently sample the cuisine of Messrs Sainsbury, St Michael and Waitrose.

The Vicar was delighted with the amount of our takings on the stall. At the end of the day he praised us before the assembled ladies of the Fête Committee, most of whom had at one time or another suffered at our hands and viewed our elevation to the great and good with an understandable mixture of outrage and suspicion.

Reaching home that evening, grubby and tired and clutching the spoils of the day to my chest, I was waylaid by my brother outside the Green Dragon.

'Mum wants you.' He was smirking in a way he knew would infuriate me. 'So move your skinny ass and get the hell inside!'

I glared. 'Push off you – you're nothing like James Cagney – more like Mickey Mouse!' and I stalked through the door with my nose in the air and a haughty expression, secretly wondering which of my many misdeeds had come home to roost *this* time.

Mother gently broke what she probably feared would be bad news; explaining that she would be returning home in a few weeks before moving to London to work for the War Office. My brother, who had been offered a post in the offices of the Blue Star Line Shipping Company until he joined the Air Force, would go with her, and it had been arranged that I should stay behind with my aunt and cousins.

'I'm sorry, darling,' she hugged me and her voice went all funny. 'You know I don't want to leave you but I shall not be able to look after you if I am working in London and it is safer for you here. I know you'll be happy with your cousins.'

It was difficult not to jump up and down with delight but I managed it, hard-hearted little wretch that I was, even squeezing a tear of two. I couldn't wait to tell Georgie. No more Mrs 'Arris grumbling, just my lovely, lovely aunt who would, I hoped, let me get away with everything short of murder. I felt that I could bear the threatened horror of Mr Mole in September if I could return each evening to her chaotic and easy-going household.

But as the Scottish Bard adjures us: 'The best laid plans of mice and men will often gang awa.' Overconfidence was to be my downfall.

* * * * *

Two weeks slipped by and Harvest was upon us. Once again the children took to the fields and I was left with Mavis and Mickey and precious little else to do but wander around the village, either with them or alone. I missed Georgie terribly; my brother, who thought and talked of little else but 'planes and flying was now far too grown-up to be a companion and I was restless and out of sorts with the world.

Miss Alice tried to console me with broken biscuits and kind words, 'Never you mind, my duck, they'm soon be back. Just wait a bit – you'll see,' and although her words comforted me a little, they were not enough to make up for the loss of Georgie's companionship.

One morning, after a squabble with the Harpers over Mavis wanting to have a Teddy Bear's tea party in the den, I stormed off home swearing never to darken their doors again until Georgie returned; Mavis backslid into respectability faster than a rat up a drainpipe.

Bored and ripe for mischief I fell back on my first love – the smuggling of the barn cats into the pub and up to my bedroom. Sitting cross-legged on my bed, playing endless games with a lure of feathers pulled across the coverlet and up and down the bed posts with two or three feral cats pouncing and tearing after in ferocious pursuit was great fun, and the fact that Mrs 'Arris would have a fit if she knew added extra spice to the games.

* * * * *

The day of reckoning came the afternoon I went down to tea and failed to notice one of the cats was still with me. As Mrs 'Arris shrieked in horror at the feline invasion I stepped back on the cat, banged my elbow on the door latch and let loose a word that made my mother blanch. Actually, it still surprises me that she knew what it meant.

There was a terrible silence. My mother's face was thunderous; my brother choked in his teacup.

'*What* did you say?'

Rooted to the spot I stayed silent. I wasn't about to dig myself any deeper.

'Where did you hear such a word?'

With unusual filial bravado my brother blundered into the breech. 'At the school probably; everyone there swears like Billy-o!'

My mother rounded on him. 'Who does? Who is *everyone*?'

He quailed, caught my anguished look and under the circumstances did the best he could. 'Old Mole, mostly,' he mumbled, 'and the kids – a bit.'

* * * * *

My mother on the warpath was an impressive sight. I doubt if Mr Mole knew quite what hit him; I imagine even he was left reeling from my mother's ladylike verbals. I wished I could have been there; I imagine it was rather like Lady Astor ripping off Winston Churchill. Miss Alice heard on the village grape-vine that she accused him amongst other things of corrupting innocent children, and gave her opinion that he was unfit to care for white mice, let alone other people's offspring.

The outcome of all this was inevitable: a few days later my bag was packed alongside my mothers and brothers. In a contest between Hitler and Mr Mole, Hitler had won hand's down.

* * * * *

I don't think Georgie and I ever really said goodbye. My remembrance is of just saying, 'Tar-rah a bit' the evening before we left The Green Dragon, then watching his sturdy figure walk to his cottage and him turning at the door to wave a brief farewell.

Mavis and Mickey promised to write and my little cousin wept copiously. *He* had been convent-educated before evacuation, so goodness knows what even my most relaxed aunt thought at her eventual discovery of his depravity: not much, I imagine. A few years later she gave him to the Christian Brothers to try and sort him out, but they never did.

* * * * *

So back we went to confront the Luftwaffe, who greeted our arrival in London with one of their less frequent but still devastating raids. We stayed overnight in Maida Vale with my mother's eldest sister and nothing will ever erase from my memory the sounds of planes and bombs and anti-aircraft batteries joined together in a non-stop, night long barrage of terror. My mother's expression as next day we picked our way over the rubble and shattered glass en route to Liverpool Street Station showed more clearly than any words that she regretted removing me from the safety of the Forest. But my hopes and prayers that she would relent and send me back remained unanswered; there were already plans afoot of which I was yet unaware.

Before the autumn term began I was dragged unwillingly to Daniel Neal's and kitted out with three of everything. Once more wearing the hated brown gymslip, brown, gold braided blazer and crowned with the familiar hideous velour pudding basin, I joined a train full of similarly attired young females heading for the South Devonshire coast, whither Miss Lee had already removed her school and pupils, lock stock and barrel.

The prison gates clanged shut again. My brief but heady freedom was over.

But there were of course compensations.

My former classmates welcomed me back and were entranced by my new skills. The roar of anti-aircraft guns were rivalled by the thunderous belches echoing from behind the tennis pavilion during break. Packets of Woodbines were acquired from the nearby town by various underhand means and many blissful hours spent deep within sheltered cliffs during nature rambles, puffing expertly and belching smoke like contented dragons – an activity that I and many of my generation had reason to regret years later, when the cigarette had taken its toll on health, but in those halcyon days it was only an almost innocent and pleasurable pursuit.

My tutorials also covered the intricacies of the Worcester-shire dialect with all of its colourful language, and visiting hockey teams would return to their own establishments bemused and bewildered by the strange-sounding oaths hissed at them when the going got rough.

I never did become Head Girl; I can't think why. I did however become a form prefect. It was a solemn moment when Miss Lee pinned the red enamelled shield to my breast. That the pin encountered a Woodie butt in the breast pocket of my gymslip and the badge shot off into the platform drapes was perhaps an unfortunate omen of things to come.

Poor Miss Lee: in spite of all her efforts and my mother's hopes, I never did become a lady. They both tried, but the

Forest, Mr Mole and Georgie Little got to me first.

For which I have been, ever and always, eternally grateful.

... and Endings

It seemed an unconscionable time before I reached sixteen and escaped to become a Junior Miss (teenagers not yet having been invented). Before that I was conscripted into the school's Girl's Training Corps where I wore a navy battledress, learned First Aid, Morse Code and how to dial telephone numbers in the dark ... don't ask, no one ever explained why or, if they did, I wasn't listening at the time. I swanked around on Church Parades, found to my surprise that uniforms were sexy, and discovered boys and it dawned upon me that there was more to being a girl than I'd previously thought. I was even in fashion at last; Shirley Temple curls were out and long sleek locks were in.

An eagle eye was kept upon us by our adjutant, Miss Wilkins, who had old lady's legs and wore long silk knickers with stout elastic below the knees. But we still managed a few clandestine meetings around the back of the drill hall; practising our first chaste and inexpert kisses on the callow and pimply Army Cadets from the boys' Grammar. However it was a long time before we managed even an approximation of what James Mason did to Margaret Lockwood in The Wicked Lady.

Later, with a fair number of cousins and my friend's brothers to choose from as escorts during school holidays, I gravitated slowly from the innocent front to the more knowledgeable back row of the cinema, becoming in the process adept at picking out the most attractive (for most attractive read least spotty) youths through one eye, the other being hidden Veronica Lake style by a hanging curtain of hair newly washed in Amami shampoo.

With two cinemas nearby and three more a short bus ride away, there was never any problem of where to go with the latest swain. Whilst repelling the more amorous advances of Sydney or Colin or Roy or whichever lucky chap had paid for the seats and the interval ice cream, I fell in love with John Mills, Michael Redgrave, Charles Boyer, Clark Gable and a host of others, counting the days to the time when I might leap out into the wide world beyond the school gates. Pursued in my imagination by John, wooed by Michael, propositioned by Charles – and even more thrillingly, carried up the staircase at Tara by Clark Gable, I lived each day in a romantic haze.

Ah, adolescence, adolescence ...

* * * * *

My mother continued whatever war work it was that kept her away from home. Our furniture remained in store and I spent my school holidays with another of my many Aunts and Uncles, and an intellectually challenged dog named Rambler. These holidays I found exceedingly irksome; the house was on the edge of the town where I knew no one else of my own age, and much as I loved dogs and longed for one of my own, as a companion Rambler was useless. If I took him for a walk he stood and glared balefully at any other dog we met, if I threw a ball he ate it, if I walked two feet ahead of him he got lost, if I *tried* to lose him he always managed to find his way home again. For the first time in my life I was totally and utterly bored. Eventually, after a great deal of wheedling and sulking and telephoning of my mother, I was allowed a holiday job in the lending library at a branch of W.H. Smith, for which I was paid the princely sum of a half-crown a week.

This was slave labour but I didn't mind the niggardly wage or having to sweep the shop floor and make the tea, because I could borrow the kind of books that, had I taken them into my own home, my mother would have found and confiscated as unsuitable. They had rather lurid paper covers and were without exception deeply romantic: full of heroines with swelling bosoms who fainted with desire at the sight of some strapping Hussar in impossibly tight breeches, or were carried off by a flashing-eyed sheikh and ravished on the desert sand. Sex, it seemed, wasn't all Emily Dripping – it also had its enjoyable side.

No sooner had I finished reading one of these enlightening tomes and returned it to the library shelves than it would be pounced upon by one of the grey-haired ladies of impeccable character and gentility who made up the bulk of our borrowers. This I found quite amazing. At sixteen, I thought grey-haired ladies were past sex and all that sort of thing.

I know better now.

* * * * *

The war dragged on. My brother came on leave from his Squadron bringing with him a blond Polish pilot who had flown one of the last 'planes out of Poland. He was half Jewish and my brother told us his parents and younger sister had been sent to a place called Auschwitz and he didn't know if they were alive or dead. He was quiet and melancholic and had beautiful eyes and I fell in love for the first time. A few weeks later he was shot down and killed over Normandy and I mourned for him in secret for many months.

* * * * *

On VE Day my friend Joyce and I fought our way up Whitehall. With the help of a Canadian Pilot we climbed onto the cross-piece of one of the lanterns outside the Admiralty to watch Churchill come out onto the balcony and wave to the crowds below. The Canadian kept shouting 'It's over, Winnie, it's over!' and we laughed and cheered with him, although Joyce's brother was still fighting with the Chindits and mine flying Mosquitoes in Burma.

But it was the end, or very nearly. I had wanted to join the Wrens and See Life, but had been born just a little too late. Now there began the returning male's patronising 'back-to-where-you-were-girls', and looming on the horizon the rationed austerity-driven fifties. Not for almost another decade, when I lived and worked in London, would I begin to taste again something of the freedom and joy and companionship that I had known in the Forest.

I often wonder what became of Mavis and Mickey and my friend Georgie, if Mavis and Mickey stayed in their Cornish village and had children to tell about the Mad Mole, and if hearing someone yell 'QUIET!' still turns their bowels to water.

If when they hear Placido Domingo sing 'You Are My Heart's Delight,' it brings back memories all the fun we had in the Des. Res.

If Georgie left his big, boisterous loving family for the wider world, or if he stayed with his roots, succumbed to some 'ole woman taking his wage packet' and now has a bevy of grandchildren who walk the path through the forest to school...

If, unlike me, those friends of my lost childhood still have someone of whom they can ask, 'Do you remember when?'

And if the gamekeeper, like his grandfather before him, still strings his victims up on the gate guarding the way through the woods, where trespassers will be prosecuted...

By the same author

And All Shall Be Well

And All Shall Be Well follows Francis Lindsey's journey through childhood to middle age; from a suddenly orphaned ten year old to a carefree adolescent; through the harsh expectations of becoming a man in a world caught in war.

Set mainly against the dramatic background of the Cornish Coast, it is a story about friendships and relationships, courage and weakness, guilt and reparation.

Paperback: ISBN: 1-931055-46-7
Hardback: ISBN: 1-931055-47-5

Available from Sagittarius Publications
62 Jacklyns Lane, Alresford, Hampshire SO24 9LH